Country Roads
~ of ~
MAINE

A Guide Book
from Country Roads Press

Country Roads
~ of ~
MAINE

Donna Gold

Illustrated by
Victoria Sheridan

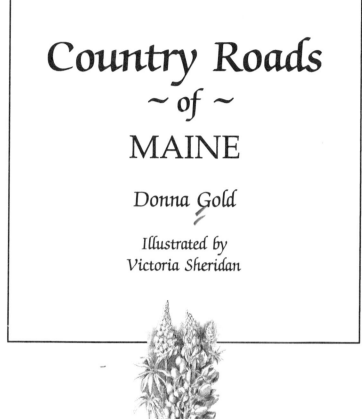

Country Roads Press
CASTINE · MAINE

Country Roads of Maine
© 1995 by Donna Gold. All rights reserved.

Published by Country Roads Press
P.O. Box 286, Lower Main Street
Castine, Maine 04421

Text and cover design by Edith Allard, Coopers Mills, Maine.
Illustrations by Victoria Sheridan.
Typesetting by Camden Type 'n Graphics.

ISBN 1-56626-070-1

Library of Congress Cataloging-in-Publication Data
Gold, Donna L.
    Country Roads of Maine / author, Donna Gold ;
illustrator, Victoria Sheridan.
        p.   cm.
    Includes bibliographical references and index.
    ISBN 1-56626-070-1 : $9.95
    1. Maine—Guidebooks.   2. Automobile travel—
Maine—Guidebooks.   I. Sheridan, Victoria.   II. Title.
F17.3.G65   1995
917.4104'43—dc20   94-23912
                                                        CIP

Printed in the United States of America.
10   9   8   7   6   5   4   3   2   1

For Daniel and for Bill,
my enduring traveling companions

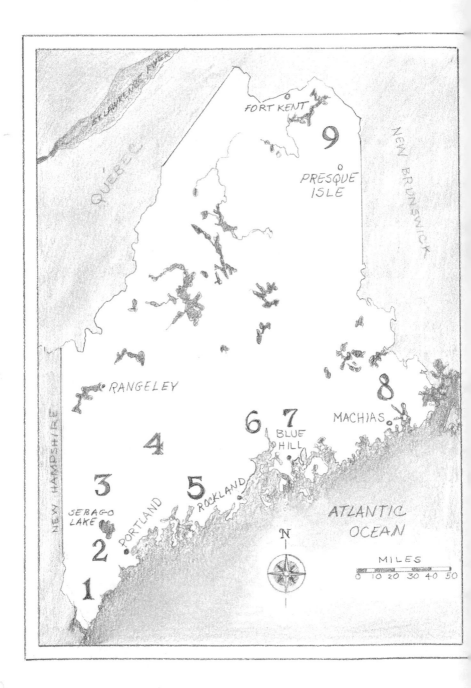

Contents

(& Key to Maine Country Roads)

Acknowledgments

Thanks first of all to Bill for his invaluable suggestions. Second, thanks to Maine's libraries, a continual resource and friendly haven, especially my two local libraries, the Buck Memorial Library in Bucksport, for friendship as well as books, and the Belfast Free Library in Belfast, which not only loaned me armloads of books but also provided the power supply for the many days I worked in its sunlit reading room.

Thanks, also, to Majo Keleshian for her companionship on a few trips, none of which quite made it into the final cut.

I also wish to thank the following newspapers for providing me with the opportunity to pursue my interests in Maine: the *Maine Times* for its pursuit of good writing about Maine, the *Waldo County Independent* for its Fireside Column, the *Kennebec Journal* for its continued belief in the arts, and the *Portland Press Herald*. Portions of some of these chapters have appeared in articles for these newspapers.

And finally there are the many, many people I have spoken with over the years, whether for this book or for other articles—people who have fallen in love with the state, or one small aspect of it, and who in pursuing their interests have become devoted experts—on the Civil War, the French and Indian Wars, the narrow-gauge railways, or the lumber industry. Sometimes the devotion takes the form of a museum, sometimes it is a book, and frequently it is a piece of art. You are among the many lights of Maine.

Introduction

It must have been six years ago that I found myself biking on the coast of Maine—I'm not sure where. Perhaps it was Winter Harbor, perhaps Sorrento. There was a house, white with a white picket fence and yellow flowers nodding on thin stalks over the fence. There were crickets clicking that quiet call that somehow makes an August day hotter, drier, more bleached. Except for those crickets, the town seemed empty, silent.

I remember the freedom of the bike's narrow wheels. I remember tears in my eyes. I remember saying something like, "I've never been so happy." That moment in that coastal town echoed my childhood dream of summer: the beauty, the stillness, the freedom. And I remember feeling surprised at my fortune, that the state where I live could so fill me.

This book is a continuation of that fortune, allowing me to put reason to my wanderings, demanding that I affix names to fleeting memories.

What do I look for when I travel here? First, there's Maine's astounding beauty, apparent almost everywhere.

Then there is the past, particularly the nineteenth-century past, which flows through so many of our children's books and so became embedded in me as my image of rural life.

Signs call to me. Collapsed wooden ships folding into the Sheepscot River in Wiscasset, schooners spreading their wings on Penobscot Bay, stone walls slinking through forests, and eruptions of trees, like weeds, in the midst of fields. Something of the pentimento of human use summons me—remnants of previous lives, of former ways.

I try also not to overlook that Maine is inhabited by a population with a fine tradition of independence: people whose ancestors were farmers, shipbuilders, sea captains, sailors, fishing folk, cabinetmakers, loggers, guides. It once took astounding physical skill to survive in this state. Think of the river runners, who once broke up logjams, balancing on floating logs while prodding at the jammed ones. That's just one highly skilled, independent occupation now gone.

On rural roads, in trailer parks, in supermarkets small and large, I see traces of the frustration with self and family that comes from the slipping away of such skills.

With that in mind, I look to understand—what life here was, is, could be.

Perhaps that is why I focus on history: it frees me to see the mutability of the landscape. When I look out my own window and find forest edging out blueberry barrens, I remember that this was recently pasturage, and where now I see an open river, sails and steamers once jostled the waters.

Art helps to understand this history—writers such as Carolyn Chute and Sarah Orne Jewett, artists such as Marguerite Zorach and Alan Bray, architects such as John Calvin Stevens or the local nineteenth-century carpenter/ farmer who nailed to his home strips of wood carved to look like Greek corner posts, transforming an old cape into a Greek Revival structure.

But to hold all the Maines I know at once in my mind is too great. Parts fall away. Ultimately, the connection is through our love of this craggy, independent, beside-the-times place—the mountains, rivers, and coast; the cities and, yes, the malls and the mills; the taciturn stubbornness and impressive openness. Time, the seasons, and the harsh rigor of Maine have tempered us all, despite ourselves.

As I finish this writing, I am startled to find my mind fashioning nine more trips. This book covers the length and nearly the breadth of the state. Some journeys take you on roads that lead to favorite destinations or through areas I cherish. Others find something unknown within a very known region. I offer a variety of things to do, though some specialties—such as fishing—I leave to the specialists. Some trips meld together several visits to an area. I confess that I have seldom done everything in one trip that I suggest can be done. Feel free to pick and choose. The lists at the back of each chapter are not exhaustive, but they do include more places than the actual trips mention.

To simplify road designations, I've used the following abbreviations: I = Interstate; US = U.S. Route or Highway; State = State Route or Highway.

I see my role here as guide, model, and student. Although these trips can be followed exactly, I hope you will pursue your own hearts and find your way down roads I didn't travel, discovering what I ignored. Let me know what I missed!

Indispensable to this book is DeLorme's *Maine Atlas and Gazetteer*, a volume of seventy maps that attempts to note every road and trail in this large state.

And there is a lot of state here. Maine's 1.2 million people are spread among 33,215 square miles. Most of the land is rural, where lighthouses outnumber cities by almost three to one.

1 ~

Textures of

the Past

in Southern

Maine's

Present

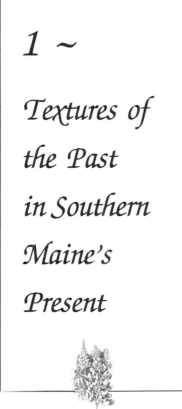

Getting there: From Portsmouth, New Hampshire, take US 1 across the Piscataqua River into Kittery, Maine. Veer off the rotary onto State 103.

Highlights: *The Portsmouth Naval Shipyard on Seavey Island in the Piscataqua River; Lady Pepperell mansion and hexagonal Fort McClary; elegant and historic buildings in York Harbor and York Village; Cape Neddick Lighthouse; the historic home of writer Sarah Orne Jewett; the Hamilton House; and the Train Man.*

Entering Maine is a celebration. Whether we are driving over the soaring bridge of I-95 or the lower Memorial Bridge on US 1, there's always a sense of disengaging, of letting go, as we head north over the Piscataqua River. It's as if Maine really were an island where life is just a little bit different, as if the rivers and mountains of New Hampshire have pushed Maine to this edge of the nation where the Atlantic laps at our toes. We have been set apart, though not exactly isolated. There's a sense of completion unto ourselves.

This first trip takes us along a coastal route through Kittery, into the Yorks, across to South Berwick, and up to

Portland via State 4. I head out on a bright September day on a family trip with Bill and our three-year-old son, Daniel.

Driving east from Kittery, we head out on a narrow road through the town's working district, passing two entrances to the Portsmouth Naval Shipyard on Seavey Island in the Piscataqua. This route circles around the elaborate mall district that has made Kittery famous and marks it as a border town. Maine may be set off from the nation, but the profusion of stores here firmly connects Kittery to the rest of the world. In some ways, this mall is a Mainer's delight, bringing the nation's material goods to our doorstep.

The shipyard adds another element: high-tech weaponry.

But even before the naval yard was commissioned, boats had been built here, numerous small boats at first, then larger boats for the British, and later, the *Ranger*, the first vessel of the Revolutionary navy. Portsmouth's modern fame has come from its submarines: the first sub, the first atomic sub, and the first Polaris missile sub built at a government-owned facility were all built here. During World War II, the shipyard employed 25,400 people. The yard stopped new construction in 1971. Today, it repairs and overhauls boats, and only 4,100 people work here. Some of the history of the yard can be found up State 236 at the Kittery Historical and Naval Museum, or at the yard itself, where historian Jim Dolph takes visitors through the museum and visitors center by appointment.

Maine frequently skids back and forth among the centuries, texturing the present with the past. We see this even as we drive. From the specter of atomic war, this winding road takes us deep into our nation's colonial days. After crossing the bridge onto Kittery Point, the road turns sharply, and we find the marks of an eighteenth-century village: a tall steepled church; a graveyard overlooking the harbor; and the elegantly decorated Georgian mansion built for Lady Pepperell, widow of the wealthy Sir William Pepperell. The mansion has limited summer hours.

The house is worth a visit for its insight into the lady who held onto her title, even after the Revolution, after much of her loyalist money was confiscated, and after the death of her husband. The battle that earned him his baronetcy occurred during the French and Indian Wars, far north on Cape Breton Island, above Nova Scotia, when William secured Louisbourg for the British crown. It reminds me how fluid boundaries really are.

Also in the enclave is Fort McClary, a hexagonal structure of thick granite and squared-off logs built on a rise at Kittery Point. There was much trouble to warrant a fort. At the time, the British and French were hotly contesting who would control the North American colonies, so the French were a worry. So were the Native Americans, especially those allied with the French. Then there were pirates. But there were also problems with the neighbors. The Kittery settlement had to fend off New Hampshire authorities who sought to tax Massachusetts vessels arriving here.

As we head into the village of Kittery Point, which competes with York as the oldest town in Maine, we pass still more colonial buildings. Then we enter the village enclave, where we find the Frisbee General Store, established in 1828. It claims to be "North America's oldest run family store." Nearby is the original Pepperell home, much more utilitarian than the Lady's and somewhat disturbed by renovations. Cap'n Simeon's Galley is a place to eat seafood overlooking Portsmouth Harbor. Also in the enclave are the town docks, looking out over a harbor full of fishing boats.

We now pass Chauncey Creek Road, following an old railway bed to the Chauncey Creek Lobster Pier, open in season. It serves no-frills lobster on the wharves where the catch comes in—a choice place to eat the tasty crustacean.

Continuing on State 103, we cross into York and meander inland among marshes before entering a long straightaway. Despite York's burgeoning population, these are relatively quiet roads.

Just before the York River Bridge we take a right on Harris Island Road, following signs for the Dockside Guest Quarters. Located on an island in York Harbor, the Dockside has exceptional views. Though we've arrived at the restaurant between meals, a waiter graciously serves us coffee and Daniel a snack.

The island backs onto a large marsh known as Wheeler Wildlife Refuge. There are no walks in the refuge, but a long, narrow suspension bridge, called the exceedingly descriptive Wiggly Bridge, leads over the waters from State 103. We stop the car to watch two egrets standing white and erect in the marsh of green and yellow reeds. As we jiggle across the bridge, a blue heron flies overhead. Eric Lusty of the Dockside says that, come late September, flocks of Canada geese gather in the marsh before their long trip south.

Back in our car, we soon meet US 1A which circles through York. The Yorks are composed of Cape Neddick, a zone of large homes on the way to Ogunquit; York Beach, a seaside town with traces of summer honky-tonk; York Village, the year-round business quarters of York, including Old York Village, a colonial restoration of historic value; the old fishing village of York Harbor, to which we are coming now; and York.

Nestled among trees on this side of the harbor is the 1718 Sayward-Wheeler House, the birthplace in 1759 of Sally Sayward Barrell Keating Wood, Maine's first novelist and the first of a full quartet of women writers we will touch upon on this trip. Her birthplace remains an unusually intact eighteenth-century home, revealing something of the life of the era. It's open to the public seasonally.

As the road curves north around York Harbor, we see elegant summer cottages, then some hotels, among them the

York Harbor Inn, and eventually the massive Anchorage Inn. York Harbor was but a farming and fishing village until prosperity brought summer visitors. As early as the 1830s, a few came to board at local farmhouses. By the late nineteenth century, they stayed at the hotels and private summer cottages that sprang up with the trade. It wasn't long before the area, with its four popular beaches, became quite the summer resort.

In the last twenty years, The Yorks have changed again. Their proximity to Boston (not much more than an hour away) has made them something of bedroom communities. Between 1970 and 1990 the population here nearly doubled.

Soon we see the impact of that growth as we head north on US 1A: campgrounds filled with trailers edging the south end of Long Beach; houses climbing over each other in typical beachside congestion along the road. We are entering the summer hurly-burly of York Beach.

Before heading into town, we take a right at the sign directing us to Cape Neddick Light, at Cape Nubble, formerly known as Savage Rock. Parking in front of a sign proclaiming "No Sunday Scuba Diving," we take a look at Cape Neddick Light, which, along with many other of the state's lighthouses, has been called "the most photographed place in Maine."

And for good reason. This bright lighthouse, topped by a red roof and separated from the cape by a steaming surf, is a cheery, stalwart place in spite of its rugged location. When the lighthouse was inhabited, the school-age children of the keeper would cross the surf each day in a basket rigged to a pulley.

Here, in 1602, early British explorers found some Native Americans in a European-style Biscay shallop with sail and oars. According to Neil Rolde's *Maine: A Narrative History*, the "lasting impression of natives in a nonnative vessel was reinforced by the costume of the chief, 'a waistcoat of black work, a pair of breeches, cloth stockings, shoes, hat and band.' "

While we ponder the past, hunger propels us headlong into the present. We turn back on US 1A, following signs to York Beach for The Goldenrod, a famous relic of a resort restaurant.

The Goldenrod is a great old beachfront restaurant and candy shop recalling the grand beach eateries of my childhood. Visitors can watch huge machine arms pull pastel-colored ribbons of saltwater taffy. Peanut brittle is made here and ice cream and sixty-five tons of saltwater taffy each season, but the best entertainment in this cavernous, one-room restaurant may be watching the sundaes pass with mouth-watering frequency—whipped cream and chocolate spilling over deep parfait glasses. We order sandwiches and frappes and are totally satisfied. My frappe—I still think of it as a milkshake—comes just as it should, in a tall glass set into a metal holder. But before we can quite finish, our three year old slips out the door. We have promised Daniel a trip to the zoo.

A child's paradise, York's Wild Kingdom Zoo and Amusement Park is just down the road. There are rides, a playground, and paddleboats as well as the zoo. Perhaps it is dated, but Daniel doesn't notice, and we don't either, though I could do without the "Mexican Hat Dance" wafting from speakers hidden behind bushes near the playground.

The zoo has one highlight for which I'd return, even without the urging of Daniel. At the far end of the grounds are tall doors where visitors can actually enter a penned area to walk among European spotted fallow deer. Like intimate friends, these Bambi-like creatures insistently snuggle our fingers for pellet treats sold for a quarter at nearby vending machines. The deer are so gentle and so numerous that their quiet, charming calm prevails over all human energies. I stand inside the pen, gazing beyond the deer at a giraffe bobbing its head as it strolls through its enclosure, and then over at the ibex with its masked face and gracefully curved horns. It is softness I note, and quiet rhythm. I feel as if I have become part deer.

We stay at the park until closing time, then return to York Village via the Ridge Road. In the York Village Historic District stands yet another portion of Maine history, a community of colonial-era buildings. Among them is the Old Gaol, or jail, built in 1719, the oldest English government building remaining in the United States. In both Jefferds Tavern, now the Old York Village visitors center, and the adjacent bench-lined schoolhouse, children may don the clothes of their historical counterparts to experience life in the 1720s.

The town is the first chartered English city in the New World (though later denigrated to a mere town), founded in 1641 upon an old Native American settlement near the river Agamenticus, later renamed the York River. This original European settlement was first called Gorgeana, after English nobleman Sir Ferdinando Gorges, who owned the charter to much of southern Maine. The name was changed to York in 1652 after the town was annexed by the Massachusetts Bay Colony. This change honors the capture of York, England, by Oliver Cromwell. On this side of the Atlantic, Gorges was on the wrong side of the dispute, losing both land and namesake.

Europeans had been fishing the waters off Maine for a number of years even before Gorgeana was charted, but they remained mostly on the outlying islands such as Monhegan and Damariscove, relatively safe from Native American attacks. But the Native Americans weren't safe from the Europeans. The simplest European infection proved fatal to them. Between 1617 and 1619, the native population dropped from an estimated 38,000 to about 5,000. With Native American life in disarray, the Europeans moved in. Still, the balance wasn't settled.

York Village surrounds a central Old Burying Ground, with stones marked by winged skulls and flowery words: "The curtain of death concealed her from mortal view." This cemetery is haunted by Candlemas Day 1692, when the Abenakis attacked the original York settlement, burning the buildings, killing from forty to seventy-five people, and leading the survivors (between 100 and 260, accounts vary) on a forced march to Canada.

It was but another battle in the so-called French and Indian Wars. For a time, the Native Americans tasted victory, the British having fled into Massachusetts, not only from York but from many settlements farther north.

But the colonists regrouped and resettled. Thirty-two years later, they led a revenge attack on the Abenaki in Norridgewock, a village high on the Kennebec River to which the assembled tribes had fled; it proved the deciding blow for the Maine Native Americans.

Leaving The Yorks, we head toward historic South Berwick by taking US 1A around the monument and left to York Village. At US 1 we turn left, head south for a moment, then turn right onto State 91, also known as South Berwick Road. We take this twining path for nine miles, crossing a branch of the York River and passing much marshland and a handful of eighteenth-century homes.

As we continue through what was once the Scottish section of York, I look on the left for the MacIntire Garrison, the oldest dated structure in the state. The building was a garrison built to defend York—then Gorgeana—against the Native Americans. The overhanging second story is typical of garrisons. Beneath the clapboard sheathing, the walls are built of logs that are nearly eight inches thick.

Just after the garrison, a white sign on the right announces Wild Iris Herb Farm. Selwyn Silberblatt, a painter, works the tractor; Lucy Clarke, a Portsmouth woman, grows the herbs—gardens of them—outside a mid-nineteenth-century cape down Kingsbury Lane. Lucy says her peak season is mid-June—lupine time—and that perennials and herbs are for sale right from the beds.

The road now moves through thick woods before returning to farmland. I think of what it must have meant for early settlers to have cleared the woods for farms and pasturage. Southern Maine was heavily lumbered in colonial days. Most of the trees were cut to build ships and cities; frequently the lumber was sailed to Boston, which had already been denuded. But the tallest, straightest trunks were cut for masts, and the thickest were reserved for the king of England. Colonists were forbidden to use any tree thicker than twenty-four inches; the king's soldiers were free to invade homes to enforce the law. Woe to any farmer with a twenty-six-inch floorboard.

Few stands of white pines now remain. This means that even northern Maine, with its acres of forests, still looks nothing like the Maine known before the first Europeans.

Near the Old McIntire Road, which comes in at the line between Eliot and South Berwick, the fields are thick with asters on this September afternoon.

In the days when passage by water was swifter than by land, South Berwick's location upriver from Portsmouth was central. A trip from Portsmouth to South Berwick would take all day by land; by river it was but a two-hour sail. Indeed, the history of Maine towns can be understood as a history of transportation. When water traffic was essential, towns sprang up along rivers and in sheltered harbors at the protruding tips of tortuous coasts. Finding these towns today— Castine, Stonington, Lubec, even Boothbay—takes a lot of driving down long peninsulas. When shipping died out, these towns frequently lost their prosperity—but not always the trappings of wealth. Throughout Maine, gorgeous nineteenth-century sea captains' homes line even the most deserted coasts.

Inland, towns grew first along the rivers. Later, the railroad came through, frequently turning settlements not blessed by a station into ghost towns. We'll see this in Paris Hill, which is preserved in its nineteenth-century splendor just because it was skirted by the railroad (see Chapter 3). When the railroad era ended, those towns suffered. Even Greenville, with the entirety of Moosehead Lake at its feet, was devastated by the loss of train travel. Greenville once packed in visitors on sleepers from Boston and New York. The auto trip lures many fewer folk.

We head into South Berwick, taking a right where State 236 links with State 91. This historic community of shipbuilders and merchants is marked by several exceptional old homes and the rich trove of stories written by Sarah Orne Jewett, native daughter of South Berwick. Her childhood home, the Jewett House, is in the center of town, across from a small traffic island.

The 1774 house would be worth a visit even without the connection to the author, for it is both elegant and homey, with fascinating old wallpaper. Jewett, who lived from 1849 to 1909, wrote from the second-story hallway beside a window overlooking the town square. Not much is changed from her day, not the crested pink wallpaper in her sister's room, which she lampooned in her story *Deephaven*, nor the windowpanes where as a child she loved to carve her initials.

But looking below, the automobile traffic circling the central square of this town of 6,000 seems to be bursting its eighteenth-century seams.

The house came into the Jewett family through the author's grandfather, Theodore Jewett, who ran away to sea as a boy and retired wealthy, having captained a ship. His stories filled Jewett's childhood, much as the furniture he bought in England and France and the trinkets he carried from the Orient filled the house. His son, Sarah's father, was a country doctor who often let Sarah skip school to accompany him on trips to farm and coast. Between her grandfather's yarns and her father's ministering, Jewett learned to listen.

"I determined to teach the world that country people were not awkward and ignorant as city people seemed to think," she wrote of her neighbors. "I wanted the world to know their grand, simple lives. So far as I had a mission when I first began to write, I think that was it."

At fifteen, Jewett was already published in the *Atlantic Monthly*. By her death, she had written more than 170 stories, mostly delicate tales of New England life such as *The White Heron* and *The Country of the Pointed Firs*.

Returning to the roads, we drive around for a while and suddenly find ourselves in New Hampshire. That reminded me of an old Maine story that Robert Ryan of the Boothbay Railway Village recounted to me. "There was a border dispute between New Hampshire and Maine that had gone on for years," he says. "Finally, after much bickering, it was resolved, and one old farmer discovered that his home was not in Maine any longer but in New Hampshire. A journalist came up to the old man to get his reaction. 'How does it feel to not live in Maine any longer?' the journalist asked the old man. 'That don't bother me,' he replied, 'I don't think I could stand another Maine winter.' "

I turn the car around, heading south on State 236 through town, following signs for Vaughan Woods.

We park in Vaughan Woods for a moment. Though there's an ancient feeling in this wood, this area was farmland before and after the Europeans arrived. The Native American tribes of this region practiced slash and burn agriculture as far north as the Saco River. It probably remained as farmland until the early twentieth century.

To get to the Hamilton House, we briefly retrace our path north, turning left as the sign indicates. This 1785 Georgian mansion was built on the spot where the Salmon Falls River takes a turn before merging with the Piscataqua River.

The first time I visited, dusk had already fallen, and this large, four-square structure looked as though it belonged to the antebellum South, not to Maine. Having arrived long past the hour the house had closed, Daniel, Bill, and I wandered among the extensive formal gardens, playing hide-and-seek with our shadows, rolling down hills and crouching behind the enclosures of boxwood hedges.

Then, in the rear of the garden we came upon a wooden cottage that seemed to have grown there. Through the tall, multipaned windows of this enchanted cottage we could see a grand piano resting upon a Persian rug. Nothing else was in the room.

On the other side of the cottage, benches lined the hill facing the river, which widens as it bends around the rear of the house. The river was absolutely still that night, reflecting the greening sky. We sat as if in another world.

Today, the tour guide is a new mother. Her young daughter rests in a pack on her back, busily flirting with the older Daniel, who squirms in my arms, protesting the tour.

Two hundred years ago, this silent turn in the river was bustling with Col. Jonathan Hamilton's wharves and warehouses. The forests, now so abundant in every direction, were simply not here, having been clipped for pasturage and shipbuilding. And this house was not built to be the quiet, wooded retreat I had fallen in love with that earlier night, but a manor house above an industrial plain.

Sarah Orne Jewett set her romantic novel The Tory Lover *in this four-square Georgian house built by wealthy merchant-shipbuilder Jonathan Hamilton*

Colonel Hamilton was born poor but made a fortune in shipping and rum-running. He had a plantation in the West Indies, worked by slaves. He also probably used slaves in his South Berwick home while he entertained the elite of the new nation. When he built Hamilton House, the Jewett house was already standing. Using that as a model, his aim was for something grander still.

Hamilton died about fifteen years after the house was built, and his family plummeted back into poverty.

For a long time, the house was owned by a farmer. It fell into disrepair until Jewett (who set her historical novel *The Tory Lover* here) persuaded friends Emily and Elizabeth Tyson, a stepmother and daughter, to buy the house as a summer retreat. Influenced by the arts and crafts movement, the Tysons filled the house with handcrafts from the turn of the century.

They also planted the extensive formal gardens, complete with shelters built into the hedges, and created the garden cottage. Jane takes us through the cottage, and I find it even more enchanting inside than I had imagined. It incorporates an early eighteenth-century building the Tysons rescued from destruction, turning the small cottage into a maze of tiny rooms, low ceilinged and stuccoed, uneven as if it were a cave, with little niches for shelves.

The Tysons entertained here. Except for Jewett, we don't know who came, but we can imagine the distinguished William Dean, a York summer resident and Jewett's editor at the *Atlantic Monthly*, also came, bringing his friends. Perhaps Jewett's friend Henry James was among them.

There are no literary salons here now, but on July and August Sundays, Hamilton House hosts informal concerts in the gardens. Should it rain, these are moved into the cottage, echoing the past.

In leaving Hamilton House, we take Old South Road back to the junction with State 91 and State 236. We jog onto

State 91 for a moment, taking a left onto Witchtrot Road as State 91 veers to the right. At the T, we take a right onto Emerys Bridge Road. About three miles down, at the corner with the one-lane Earl's Road, marked by a cemetery, lives another South Berwick author. Gladys Hasty Carroll is in her nineties now; her *As the Earth Turns* was a best-seller of the 1930s. The nonfiction *Dunnybrook* was also popular. Carroll, who opened her book *Years Away from Home* with the line, "In the beginning was The House," still lives beside the house of her own beginnings.

This house, built by her grandfather, is open to visitors during "Welcome Days" held on consecutive weekends in mid-July. Carroll, a delightful woman, joins several of her contemporaries in offering tours of the historic homestead and surrounding region. Several times each day, Carroll's granddaughter, Carrie Jones, and her husband, Jeff, perform skits they've created from passages in *Dunnybrook*, using the fields, cemeteries, and parts of the home as backdrops.

Several years ago, I visited Carroll. She spoke of her childhood in this back road off a back road: "At night, after the work was done, I remember my grandmother and her daughters—and I was there, too—would sit around the kitchen table with the one kerosene light, and my grandmother would read, and all the women would gather around, trying to get close to the light to see their sewing and mending."

The women would read the Bible, Dickens, the Brontes, and Jewett. These nightly readings in the most remote of farmhouses were not rare in Maine. Historians and historical accounts frequently speak of the literateness of the nineteenth-century Maine farmer.

At North Berwick Road, we turn left toward North Berwick and an inland route (State 4) to Portland.

Bypassing Sanford, we drive through Alfred, a historic town that looks like a furniture center. Actually, the illusion is the work of just one man, John Folsom, Sr., who took over a family furniture business begun in 1898 in Springvale, with a dream of displaying furniture in a home setting. He now has three homes where he shows furniture, one being the home of a former county judge, another being the nineteenth-century York County Jail.

Next to the home where the mattresses are displayed stands the Holmes House, a private home built by Maine's first senator, John Holmes. Across the top of the building Holmes placed wrought-iron bows and arrows. "He had the arrows pointed down," says John Folsom, Sr., "to show friendliness with the Indians."

The historic Olde Berry Inn, just off State 4A, still welcomes guests.

North of Alfred, on a hill over Shaker Pond, stands Notre Dame Apple Orchards. Here, from Labor Day through mid-October, visitors can pick apples rooted in religion. For 140 years a Shaker community lived here, later merging with the New Gloucester community (see Chapter 2). When the Shakers left, the Brothers of Notre Dame moved in. Though the orchards are now managed by the younger blood of Gile Orchards, the Brothers still live on the hill, and welcome those who wish to talk, or visit their church, gardens, and monastery.

We now pass through Waterboro and East Waterboro into Hollis Center, which earned the name Rope Walk because it was so long and narrow, like the buildings used to spin rope from manila hemp.

At State 117 we briefly leave State 4 and bear right toward Salmon Falls. We take a left after a little more than two miles, just before the bridge over the Salmon Falls River. A red library stands on our right.

Here the road narrows and bends as if after 150 years it has settled into the ground. All the homes in this riverside enclave are elegant, but the most grand is probably the third house on the left, Quillcote, the home of Kate Douglas Wiggin (1856–1923), author of *Rebecca of Sunnybrook Farm*. A quill weathervane above the red barn arches toward the sky.

Kate and her younger sister used to ride the logs feeding into a local sawmill on the river, jumping off just before the lumber got to the circular saw. Kate grew up in a nearby home, and always longed for this old colonial house.

Like Jewett and Carroll and other rural Maine children of that broad era, Wiggin was raised reading. By age twelve, as she writes in her diary, she had read nearly every book of Charles Dickens, "and some of them six times." Then, when Dickens was traveling through New England on a reading tour, she met the great man on a train headed for Portsmouth. The diary excerpt continues:

"I planted myself breathlessly and timorously down, an unbidden guest, in the seat of honor. . . . I was frightened, but not so completely frightened as if I had been meeting a stranger. You see I knew him even if he did not know me."

Having initiated a conversation with Dickens, the twelve-year-old girl mentions that when she does read his books, "I do skip some of the very dull parts once in a while; not the short dull parts, but the long ones." Dickens proceeds to engage her in a charmed literary examination of his own dullness, followed by a discussion of which were the saddest portions of his novels, and whether she and he cried at the same passages, until the train pulls into the station.

Kate's family eventually left Hollis for California, but she later returned, first to rent, then to buy her dream home, complete with a fresco by the man known as the Yankee Wall Painter, Rufus Porter. She named the house Quillcote, to mean the house of the pen. Wiggin spent summers here, working in a woodland study with forest wallpaper, moss green carpeting, and long French windows to let the woods in. The home is not currently open to the public.

We follow this riverside road north past a country club to State 4 where we turn right toward Bar Mills. But we don't quite leave Wiggin territory. On our right on State 4, close to the bridge that leads from the Hollis section of Bar Mills to the Buxton section of Bar Mills, stands a large brick home with a sign out front announcing The Train Man.

Here, in the region once associated with two railroad inventors—Freeman Hanson, who devised the locomotive turntable, and Silas G. Smith, who created the locomotive snowplow—lives model train buff John V. Raser, who goes by the name of Jack. He has spent the past twenty-one years turning the entire basement of his tall brick house into an elaborate miniature world where thumb-sized hikers climb mountains and sophisticated urbanites mill outside of a miniature and politically very incorrect "xxx"-rated show, all within a feather's throw of one of a host of model rail lines. It is quite a setup, with the lines weaving mazelike around the basement's myriad vents, ducts, and heaters.

All this has nothing to do with the claim to fame of the house itself, which is as the setting for *Rebecca of Sunnybrook Farm*. The aunt with whom Rebecca goes to stay is supposed to have lived here, in the home of one of Wiggin's closest friends.

The Train Man also sells model railroad equipment from his basement.

We are now quite close to Portland. We cross the bridges over the Saco River in Bar Mills, continuing straight past the temptation to turn off for State 4 and US 202, and take the Portland Road. It joins with State 22 through a mixture of rural and suburban homes. After North Scarborough, we see a gaggle of geese squawking on our left. Smiling Hill Farm, a child-accessible farm with a playground and other facilities, rises on the hill above.

The route now passes the executive parks of several Portland industries and Portland's historic Stroudwater district before depositing us onto Congress Street.

In the Area

Kittery Historical and Naval Museum, Kittery, 207-439-3080.

Portsmouth Naval Shipyard historian Jim Dolph, Kittery, 207-438-3550.

Lady Pepperell House, Kittery Point.

Fort McClary, Kittery Point, 207-439-2845.

Frisbee General Store, Kittery Point, 207-439-0014.

Cap'n Simeon's Galley, Kittery Point, 207-439-3655.

Chauncey Creek Lobster Pier, Kittery Point, 207-439-1030.

Dockside Restaurant and Guest Quarters, York, 207-363-2868.

Sayward-Wheeler House, York Harbor, 603-436-3205 or 207-363-2709.

Cape Neddick Inn, Cape Neddick, 207-363-2899.

The Goldenrod, York Beach, 207-363-2621.

York's Wild Kingdom Zoo and Amusement Park, York Beach, 800-465-4911.

Old York Historical Society, York Village, 207-363-4973 or 207-363-4974.

Wild Iris Herb Farm, York, 207-363-4153 in season; 603-335-2375 off season.

Sarah Orne Jewett House, South Berwick, 603-436-3205 or 207-384-1945.

Vaughan Woods, South Berwick, 207-384-5160.

Hamilton House, South Berwick, 603-436-3205 or
   207-384-5269.

The Counting House, South Berwick, 207-384-8041.

Dunnybrook Historical Society Welcome Week, South
   Berwick, 207-384-1940 (June through July only), or
   207-384-2263.

Folsom's, Alfred, 207-324-5800.

Olde Berry Inn, Alfred, 207-324-0603.

Gile Orchards, Alfred, 207-324-2944.

The Train Man, Bar Mills, 207-929-3621.

Smiling Hill Farm, Stroudwater, 207-775-4818, or
   207-775-2408.

Tate House, Stroudwater, 207-774-9781.

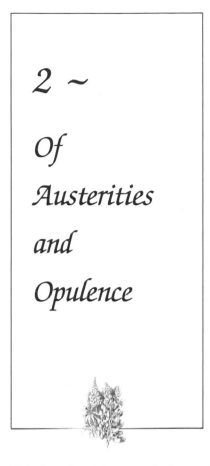

2 ~

Of

Austerities

and

Opulence

Getting there: Take I-295 north through Portland to the first Falmouth exit. Go about 1.5 miles and turn left onto State 9 west.

Highlights: *The Shaker village at Sabbathday Lake; the Poland Spring House, in the 1800s a resort of legendary elegance; the State of Maine building from the 1893 World's Columbian Exposition in Chicago; the oldest Quaker meetinghouse in Maine; and the boyhood home of Nathaniel Hawthorne.*

This is a day trip, wandering not far from Portland, though for a longer journey this can be linked to the journey in Chapter 3, which leads to Norway, South Paris, Paris Hill, and the Norlands Living History Center. Besides being a luscious drive during any season, these quiet, lesser-used roads close to Portland lead to a series of unusual places in southern Maine, including the consciously humble Shaker village and the self-consciously grandiose establishments around Poland Spring.

It is mid-June and I am traveling on State 9 west with my son, Daniel. Before long, we are in true countryside. As if to emphasize this, we are halted by a train at the railroad intersection of State 9 and the Range Road, within sight of the Farmer's Co-op. We watch as thirty-six cars pass. Most are container cars, among them one labeled caustic soda. By the time the five final coal cars pass (sadly, without a final caboose), Daniel has been lulled to sleep. Later, I realize that this is a historic route, part of the Grand Trunk Railway, which opened in 1853 and once connected Portland and Montreal.

Driving through Cumberland Center beneath the afternoon's graying sky, we pass many weathered gray houses caving in upon themselves, looking like hobbled old women burdened by age and care.

This area was settled early and grew to some prominence. According to one of my favorite historical reference books, George Varney's 1881 *Gazetteer of the State of Maine*, which describes Maine settlements alphabetically town by town, Cumberland was a thrifty town and home to "much mental culture . . . notable for the many distinguished persons—ministers, missionaries, authors and teachers, who were born or have lived there."

From Cumberland, the road ascends to Walnut Hill, where State 9 branches northeast. We continue north on State 115/State 231 for about 1.5 miles until they separate, then bear right on State 231, the New Gloucester Road.

We pass several massive chicken barns with their rows of holes where the vents used to be. These barns, however old they seem, speak to a rather recent era when poultry was the largest farming commodity in the state, worth $98 million in 1966, pushing even potatoes to second place.

Barns such as these once housed 8,000 to 10,000 egg layers, the eggs usually marketed in Boston. Broilers were also raised in these huge sheds, which looked more like factories than farms. Then in the late 1970s, the energy crisis made

it too costly to ship feed from the Midwest to the Northeast, and the poultry industry consolidated in the South,
partially because the southern processors were not union-
ized. Exacerbating the problem may have been a certain slug-
gishness on the part of the Maine processors to market their
chickens.

The loss was devastating to areas around Lewiston,
where we'll be passing today, as well as to the Belfast region,
which we pass in the journey in Chapter 5. Many of the
chicken barns have been scrubbed down and rescued from
oblivion, however—turned into artists' studios and potters'
sheds, commercial storage units, a music studio housing
radio WERU, and the Big Chicken Barn on US 1 near Ellsworth, now stuffed with antiques and old books.

As we drive up State 231, the old farms with their barns
trailing behind are interspersed with new ranch homes standing smart and cool on a wide expanse of mowed lawn. This is
a transitional landscape; though there are still many old structures, we are close enough to the Portland region to see new
growth and new construction.

What makes Maine special to the back-roads driver is
how little modern construction is visible. The population
pressure is not very intense here. There are only 40 people per
square mile in Maine. Even if we consider a more realistic
count that eliminates Maine's vast tracts of uninhabited forest, there are still only 200 people per square mile. Massachusetts, by comparison, has an average of 765 people living on
each square mile. And because rural Maine had such a strong
nineteenth-century life, remaining rather quiet in this century, the architecture prominent when an area was first settled—or when it found prosperity—endures, even now.

Between homes, buttercups fill the fields with a yellow
light. Above us, trees arch high above the telephone wires,
shading the road.

Soon after passing the fortress-like Pineland Center, a state institution for the mentally retarded, State 231 becomes one of the loveliest of country roads, sheltered by tall trees and crossed by railroad tracks on a wooden-planked bridge. Nearing New Gloucester, there's an unusual frequency of brick homes. Brick is not a common building material in Maine, perhaps because of the abundance of wood. But the soil is particularly thick with clay in this region, marking the edge of an ancient ocean.

The first settlers arrived in New Gloucester in 1735 from Gloucester, Massachusetts. But like many settlements established before the end of the bloody French and Indian Wars, these were soon abandoned. By the 1750s, however, Mainers began pushing back, and many areas were resettled, including New Gloucester. In 1753, the colonists returned, building a blockhouse which served as a home, fort, and church. When a meetinghouse was finally built, the pulpit doubled as a gunpowder storehouse. That meetinghouse stood until 1838.

New Gloucester now has a large historic district that includes a worthy town hall and a library painted classic yellow. The many fine two-and-a-half-story houses prove the prosperity of this farming community. For a time New Gloucester gained prestige by serving as a half-shire town with Portland. Today, this classic New England town is a bedroom community, accessible to Portland and Lewiston-Auburn. It is also known for the Shaker village at Sabbathday Lake, where we are headed, a few miles north and west of New Gloucester's center.

To get to Sabbathday Lake, we continue on State 231 to the junction of US 202/State 100/State 4. At the stop sign, we cross US 202 to Hershey Road, near the Cumberland Lodge, and make a left after the 1783 house. We are now on Snow Hill Road, a new road cut through a forest. After crossing a bridge over the Maine Turnpike and then passing swampland to the left, we turn right to Outlet Beach on the northern tip of Sabbathday Lake.

There's a little campground here with a beach one must pay to use. It's a typical Maine lakeside spot, with children splashing in the water, and inner tubes, paddleboats, rowboats, canoes, and kayaks for rent.

Maine is full of lakes—"a mirror broken into a thousand fragments," wrote one contemporary of Thoreau. These were gouged out by the retreating glacier of the last ice age and then filled by the melting waters. The lakes may have once been glacial, but their warm and slithery waters cannot compare to the bracing ting of Maine's frigid coastal waters.

Lining the road near the beach is a lakeside community of "camps," the Maine word for a small summer home, usually by a lake or river. This road revels in the age-old contentment of summer. Going to a family camp is an old Maine tradition, even among families of modest means. Those of us who endure the winter here know we deserve our summer luxuries.

Seeing these uninsulated wooden cabins reminds me of the cabin that framed my first experiences in Maine, a summer camp for girls, only about fifteen miles west of here. Being a hopeless athlete, I was quite unhappy there. Yet something about those summers, about the silence of the tall pine trees, stayed with me: here I am, ten years in Maine.

At State 26, I take a left, landing me immediately in the Shaker community of Sabbathday Lake, founded in 1783. The first Shaker image I see is a large gray granite tombstone inscribed only as The Shakers. This suffices for all members of this self-effacing, spiritual group.

The community may be small but it is still active, home to ten permanent residents: two brothers, six sisters, a museum director, and one student of the practice. One must study

The Shaker community at Sabbathday Lake still has members today

Shaker ways for five years before joining the society, which demands of its members three C's: celibacy, communalism, and confession.

To the outsider, the community is both protected and accessible, guarded and friendly. The members themselves stay in the background while opening two stores and some of their buildings to visitors and passing on their wisdom through many books and several workshops.

One store, located on State 26, offers many small, simple, Shaker-made items and some herbs and books and is open through December. Down a short hill, there's a more abundant store within a small museum, open only in summer. Here are sold more books, yarn, herbs, teas, and furniture reproductions. But the bounty is the Shaker herbology. Apparently, the Shakers nursed the Native American sick and tended to their babies; in return they were taught herb-healing and basketry, two arts the Shakers pursue to this day.

Their extensive gardens include a large herb plot. The attics hang with drying herbs.

I sign up for a tour of the village, which takes about an hour.

Carrying a sleeping Daniel in my arms through an unexpected sun shower, I hike uphill to the meetinghouse. This is a large rectangular room, noticeably cool and clean, with wide pine floorboards. The white walls are crossed by beams and wooden strips painted indigo blue, holding pegs. The blue remains bright after 200 years, without fading, flaking, or wearing thin. In the early days, the benches that now fill the room were not here, leaving space for dancing and marching. It was this free-form dancing that gave the Shakers their name. Later, the dancing became more organized; still later it was dropped. Now, meetings consist of song, Bible reading, and testimony. Meetings are open to the public on Sunday at 10:00 A.M., right here where the composer of the hymn " 'Tis a Gift to Be Simple" lived.

The Shaker faith began with Mother Ann Lee, who believed that divinity could be found within one's self. She sought to live the life of Jesus, which she saw as a simple life, filled with prayer, work, and love for others. Her phrase "Hands to work, hearts to God" is a motto of the community.

But to the Shakers' initial three C's, I would add three more: cleanliness, creativity, and craft. The Shakers see cleanliness, together with work, as a form of worship. They also know about the spiritual nature of spare beauty. Furniture and built-in cabinets are stained with vegetable dyes of mustard, indigo, or blueberry; contrasted with the white walls, these natural colors convey an unusual liberation, a simple, earthy counterpart to the great Gothic cathedrals of Europe.

This simplicity is also modern. Walking through these rooms, I hear the music of Aaron Copland's *Appalachian Spring*

Oval Shaker boxes

and envision most un-Shakerlike dancers performing spare, stretched moves against this simple, uplifting backdrop of strong color fields.

Shaker creativity also sings in the many inventions attributed to the society, including the first washing machine, circular saw, waterproof cloth, clothespin, flat broom, ladder-back chair, built-in cabinets, and horse-drawn mowing machine.

We leave by taking State 26 north to look at the Poland Spring House, an extreme contrast in human experience.

But to mediate the change and provide one of Maine's most delicious treats, we detour left at the corner of State 26 and State 122, driving a quarter-mile down the Range Hill Road—pronounced "rang"—to pick up some strawberries at the Chipman farmstand.

Young farmer Doug Chipman runs the farm his ancestors began in 1781. This was a dairy farm before he took it over, but like most contemporary farmers, he has had to diversify. Now the farm operates three farm stands and offers pick-your-own strawberries between the end of June and mid-July. Come October, there's a Halloween extravaganza here, with hayrides, an extensive pumpkin patch, mazes, and a haunted house, open weekends.

We continue north by taking the next right onto Carpenter Road, then a left onto State 26 for the Poland Spring House with its separate benches for Republicans and Democrats.

At the turn of the century, the Poland Spring House was a resort of legendary elegance. The "dining service once had the ordered precision of the Rockettes, even to the white-gloved busboys," says *Maine: A Guide Downeast*, a 1937 Works Project Administration–sponsored guide to Maine that was updated in 1970 and is still a most insightful, caring, and comprehensive guide to the state.

The hotel had been operational since the eighteenth century. In the mid–nineteenth century, the Poland springs of bottled-water fame were discovered and touted as a cure for a range of ailments, including diseases of the liver, kidneys, and bladder, and kidney stones, dropsy, salt rheum, and scrofula humors. By the 1890s, some 450 guests could take the waters within luxurious accommodations, served by more than 300 employees. Nearby was one of the earliest and best golf courses in the state. And from down the road, the simple Sabbathday Shakers would come to this watering hole selling herbs, candies, baskets, and even their distinctive capes.

Then the hotel closed and the buildings saw a succession of twentieth-century activity. They spent some time as a training school for underprivileged girls under President Johnson's Great Society, then became a center for transcendental meditation classes by the Maharishi Mahesh Yogi. A fire destroyed the building in 1975, after which new buildings were built. The resort was resurrected as a hotel, but modern casualness has taken over from the Gay Nineties opulence.

Up the hill from the hotel stands another Maine relic, a Queen Anne–style, octagonal stone structure that was the State of Maine building at the 1893 Columbian Exposition in Chicago. Its construction displays Maine's multitude of gifts: the edifice of granite from across the state, and the roof from Monson slate. It was built in Chicago with the expectation that it would remain there, but somehow it got slated for destruction. Hearing this, Hiram Ricker, the wealthy owner of the Poland Spring House, bought the building and had it dismantled, loaded onto a sixteen-car train, and brought to Poland Spring. It now holds images of the Chicago exposition and artifacts of the old Poland Spring House. Its hours are limited.

From here we return to State 26 north and cross the causeway between Middle and Lower Range Ponds, noting the gorgeous red shingle home at the causeway, a remnant of Poland Spring's heydey, for this was the hotel's bathhouse. We drive about three miles, until we are almost into the town of Poland, and take a left at the crossroads onto White Oak Hill Road. This lovely back road takes us along fields crusted with stones through to State 11. We head south into Webb Mills on Dumpling and Coffee Ponds, and we find another Maine institution—yards crowded with chicken pens and car parts. One of the ponds can be viewed through the trees.

Hiram Ricker transported the octagonal State of Maine building, built for the 1893 World's Columbian Exposition in Chicago, to the grounds at Poland Spring

Shortly after State 11 crosses State 121, we take a left onto Quaker Ridge Road en route to South Casco. This is one of Maine's gorgeous ridge roads, with a view west to Long Lake and the White Mountains in the far distance. Grazing among some mossy rocks beneath a high-voltage line are Belted Galloways—black cows with great white belts around their middles. These distinctive-looking prime beef cattle were first imported from Scotland in the 1950s by a Rockport farmer. Passing an old Friends' meetinghouse, I see why this route is called Quaker Ridge Road. The Friends Meeting House, built in 1814, is said to be the oldest in Maine. The guidebook *Maine's Historic Places,* a compilation of all the properties on the National Register of Historic Places, calls the modest meetinghouse "a remarkable survival," referring to the fact that the structure is almost entirely original. This small structure has a cut in its facade so men and women could enter separately.

This rural, historic road leads to one of Maine's busiest summer arteries, US 302 between Portland and the Sebago Lake area. But we don't venture onto this road yet, stopping just short of it at the corner, where the Cry of the Loon straddles both sides of US 302. The store is a gift shop, gallery, sculpture garden, toy store, and all-around purveyor of the brightly colored and the handmade, from food to fine art.

The store is a series of close, mazelike rooms. Upstairs, outside, and across the street is a luxurious amount of space given over to paintings, sculpture, and sculptural furniture such as an alligator-based coffee table and a beetle end table. The current show has a theme of animals, with the work ranging from humorous to iconic, representing about a dozen very good Maine artists. Since my visit, the shop has hired curator Grant Jacks, a man with a wide-ranging imagination, so the selections, compelling as they are now, can only improve.

Nearby is the Migis Lodge, a classic summer resort on Sebago Lake.

Behind the Cry of the Loon is a historic district where the boyhood home of Nathaniel Hawthorne stands among some lovely nineteenth-century houses. To get there, we leave the main building of the Cry of the Loon (the one on the Sebago Lake side), turn right onto US 302, and take an immediate right onto Hawthorne Road on Raymond Neck.

This is not Hawthorne's birthplace. He was born in 1804 in Salem, Massachusetts. But after his father, Captain Hawthorne, died in Surinam, when the author was a small child, Hawthorne's mother decided to move her three children near her brother, Richard Manning, in what was then the village of Raymond and is now South Casco. Manning was the wealthy owner of the local store. He built for himself a home with eight fireplaces, Belgian glass windows, and a preponderance of wallpaper that earned the house the name of "Manning's Folly."

For his widowed sister and her children, he built a barn-like home that some visitors have called bleak, though I don't find it so, and neither did Hawthorne, who writes that he spent his happiest days tramping through the lakeside forest of this little enclave. Indeed, he later wrote, "I have visited many places called beautiful in Europe and the United States but have never seen the place that enchanted me like that flat rock from which I used to fish." The flat rock is probably north of the little bridge over Dingley Brook, toward Thomas Pond.

Hawthorne remained here until he attended Bowdoin College in Brunswick. Like Sarah Orne Jewett and many another teller of tales, he began gathering stories early, his imagination fed by the conversations of farmers and travelers at his uncle's store. His boyhood diaries are filled with

these stories; some found their way into Hawthorne's publications, such as the ghost-telling peddler Dominicus Jor-
dan, who became Dominicus Pike in *Mr. Higginbotham's
Catastrophe.*

The Hawthorne house, at the juncture of Hawthorne and
Raymond Cape Roads, has a small sign indicating it as
Hawthorne's boyhood home. It is open to the public seasonally, by appointment. Or you can ask for a key at the small
general store next to the home. Since it now serves as a community hall, there is not much inside, except for some information on the author.

"Manning's Folly" is across Dingley Brook from the
Hawthorne House, a white structure about two houses down.

The rest of this enclave is also interesting. It's built like
an old village, with houses every which way, not laid
out along a road. Near the little brook where Hawthorne
fished is a lovely board-and-batten home (with siding of vertical wood boards). Farther down the cape is a large cliff
known as Frye's Leap. In a cave below the cliff is where
Hawthorne is said to have written the first chapter of *The
Scarlet Letter.*

I haven't seen the cave, since the point is privately
owned, but a local historian, Daphne Winslow Merrill, describes the spot in her 1973 book *The Lakes of Maine.*

> The opening was created by a fissure which became
> covered by debris and sheltered by natural growth. At
> the entrance, the dark water is deep and swirls weirdly
> in perpetual shadows. At the farther end of the narrow
> cave-like structure lies a narrow beach, lighted from
> above by some sort of opening in the rock, providing a
> magical aura. The place is often called "Hawthorne
> Cave," for the young author spent many hours in its
> shelter, drifting in his skiff.

This place abounds with legends. Out on Frye Island are paintings on Image Rocks, also known as Frye's Leap. Captain Frye, a man who made hunting the local tribes his calling, was once chased out onto this very neck by some of the men he was hunting. He ran to the cliffs, leaped from the top of the rocks to the snow covering the frozen lake below, and then ran across to the nearby island, giving both cliff and island his name.

There are fading remains of paintings on these rocks, including images of Frye taking his leap. There may also have been some old Native American pictographs here. Later, they became part of a touristic advertising stunt to get people to take a steamer around Sebago Lake. The same steamship company also hired a man to dress as an Indian and dance on the rock while the steamship passed by. Try renting a boat at a nearby marina to further explore these rocks.

I end this trip here. US 302 south is a speedy route back to Portland and a major north-south highway. There is more exploration that can be done around here, however, not the least of which is Sebago Lake—fourteen miles long, as much as eleven miles wide, and host to thousands of visitors who boat and play and fish in its waters. Sebago means "stretch of water" to the Wabanaki, and to Portland residents, who draw their water from here, relying on the cold depths of the lake—up to 400 feet deep—to assure its purity. A further exploration is the Songo Locks, a left off US 302, following signs for this historic monument.

The next trip, to Paris Hill and Norlands Living History Center, picks up near here, up the Quaker Ridge Road (lovely enough to warrant a second visit). To begin that trip, head north on US 302, turn right on State 11, and take a left within a mile at Pike Corner onto State 121 North to Casco.

In the Area

Shaker Museum, Museum Shop, and Shaker Store, New Gloucester, 207-926-4597.

New Gloucester Library

Chipman Farms, Poland Spring, pick-your-own strawberries, 207-998-4391 or 998-2027.

Maine State Building and All Souls Chapel, Poland Spring, 207-998-4142.

The Inns at Poland Spring, Poland Spring, 207-998-4351.

Cry of the Loon, South Casco, 207-655-5060.

Hawthorne House, South Casco, 207-655-3349 or 207-655-3559.

Migis Lodge, South Casco, 207-655-4524 (summer); 207-892-5235 (winter and spring).

The Olde House, Raymond, 207-655-7841.

Cruise on *Songo River Queen*, Sebago Lake, 207-693-6861.

3 ~

Changing Fortunes in the Oxford Hills

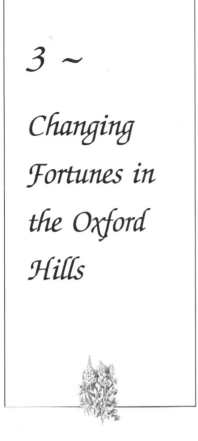

Getting there: Take I-495 (the Maine Turnpike) to exit 11 (Gray). Follow US 202 south, then State 115 to North Windham. Turn north on US 302.

Highlights: *The elegant statesmen's community of Paris Hill and the hands-on farm community at Norlands Living History Center; the Celebration Barn, home of new vaudeville theater; a visit to a sheep farm and a pick-your-own apple orchard; hiking on Streaked Mountain; and gem hunting in the western foothills.*

Traveling by any back road in Maine frequently becomes a voyage to the past, a journey to a time of self-sufficiency when barns were built right onto homes. These large farmhouses joined to their even larger barns are ever-present in central and southern Maine, even as newer homes sneak onto fields between farms. Yet though we see these places almost daily, few people know what's on the inside, or can imagine the nature of the lives once lived within.

This voyage combines two historical destinations, the elegant farm and statesmen's community of Paris Hill and the Norlands Living History Center of Livermore Falls, where history is not just seen, but experienced. The relationship between these towns stretches back almost 200 years, when Oxford County encompassed what is now both Oxford and Androscoggin Counties. At the time, Paris Hill and Livermore Falls were rivals for the county seat. Paris Hill won. Though the decision was made sometime before 1805, the impact is still apparent in the visibly decreasing affluence as we drive north from Paris Hill to Livermore Falls.

Depending on the season, there are other stops along the way. Near Paris Hill stands a world center for new vaudeville theater, the Celebration Barn, open summer through October. Come autumn, there are apples to pick at one of several local orchards. In winter, there's cross-country skiing. Gem hunting in West Paris is possible in most seasons, as is a hike up Streaked Mountain.

I begin this voyage where the journey in Chapter 2 ends, in South Casco. As we drive past stone walls that in this century divide forests instead of fields, the western horizon is marked by the Presidential Range of the White Mountains, snowcapped except in summer.

These stone walls snaking throughout the state are testimony not only to the farmers' industry and the rocky soil the farmers tilled, but to other hardships as well. Even as Maine was being settled, it suffered mass emigrations of farmers seeking greener pastures elsewhere, especially in 1816, when snow fell during every single month and a great wave of people simply gave up, leaving for Ohio and points west.

Writes Neil Jorgensen in his *Guide to New England's Landscape*, a quite readable geographic history of New England:

> One by one they abandoned the farms that only a generation or so earlier they had hacked from the wilderness. They moved to better lands farther west or into the valley towns to work in the mills. By the 1860s

the exodus from the New England hill farms had become almost a stampede. There were no takers for these abandoned farms and they quickly fell into decay. The houses and barns disappeared and fields grew up to woods. Except for the stone walls stretching for miles through the woods and an occasional gnarled old apple tree growing improbably among the pines, there is now little to indicate that much of the land was ever inhabited.

At State 11, we turn right, then in about a mile we turn left onto State 121 at Pike Corner.

The road here parallels Parker Pond, a teardrop squeezed from the larger Pleasant Lake, just beyond Casco. We take advantage of the road turnoffs to see vistas over the pond that are otherwise blocked by waterside dwellings.

I first saw this pond from the sprawling home of Martin Dibner, novelist, artist, and man of great heart, who lived on top of Mayberry Hill, on the other side of Pleasant Lake. One of his last publications before his death in 1991 was *Portrait of Paris Hill*, a tribute to the classic enclave where we're now headed.

In Casco, my son sees Pear's ice-cream stand, so we stop for a tall, wobbly cone, then continue north on State 121. This quiet, lovely road passes pine and deciduous forests, before entering Otisfield, a small, compact town with the special Maine mixture of nineteenth-century Greek Revival homes and twentieth-century mobile homes. Stone walls border forests and careen through fields. Were we to take a walk in these woods, we'd probably encounter at least one semiorderly collection of stones signifying an old house foundation.

Or perhaps foundations, for as we see along this road, nineteenth-century Mainers typically built a small house, then, as prosperity increased, attached larger living quarters onto the original structure. If they built during the mid–nineteenth century, they would have added a summer kitchen behind the house, which might also contain a work-room, leading to a shed and finally a barn, hence the circus train of houses known by the nursery rhyme: "big house, little house, back house, barn." In a book by that name, architect Thomas C. Hubka reveals the social history behind Maine house construction.

The common explanation for the attached barns is that they eased winter chores: farmers did not have to face the bitter winds to feed their animals. But this setup, which was a serious fire hazard, had other rationales. The attached outbuildings were frequently oriented so that a south- or west-facing yard could be sheltered between house and barn. This would be a place for a kitchen garden, an outdoor work area, and a relatively warm yard for young children to play near where adults were working. Equally important, this setup eased the integration of the numerous home indus-tries of the nineteenth century. The women's industries extended from the kitchen or summer kitchen (commonly an ell behind the house). The men's work gravitated from the barn to the shed. Thus men and women would be working together in the yard, or near each other in the outbuildings between house and barn—little house, back house, summer kitchen, or shed. This was the era of home industry as well as farming. To survive, farm families were also blacksmiths and tanners, carpenters and coopers. They produced butter and cheese as well as milk, preserved their food, made candles, soap, cloth, and clothing, and sold what they didn't need at home.

The attached barn arrangement is similar across the state. Indeed, the view from one of my writing haunts, the Belfast Free Library, includes a Victorian big house, little house, back

A Maine "big house, little house, back house, barn"

house, and barn in downtown Belfast. As we travel through Maine, we find that even the most ornate houses, such as the Paris Hill homes and the Washburn homestead that we come to at the end of this trip, have their practical tails of work sheds and attached barns. Generally, the farther from the home, the plainer the structure. Most barns have no architectural detail, though some may be touched by hints of the farmhouse decoration.

Beyond Otisfield at Gould Corner (where the Bolsters Mills Road veers in from the southeast) stands the Nutting Homestead, an early nineteenth-century farm that has been occupied and added to by five continuous generations of the Nutting family and is now on the National Register of Historic Places.

The fairly sizable cape section facing the road, with one story overhung by a steep roof, is from 1796, when Nathan Nutting of Groton, Massachusetts, arrived here. His son, Nathan, Jr., studied architecture in Boston and returned to

41

Otisfield in 1820 to build the Federal-style section on the cape's north side for the family of his brother, Lyman.

When Lyman married, the Nutting household had two families and two active kitchens, one per house. When Lyman's youngest son, Albert, married in the 1870s, he added the ell behind the cape, consolidating both kitchens into one. Lyman Nutting had died, and his aging wife was too ill to maintain her own kitchen.

But for reasons of their own, the Nuttings did not construct this final kitchen so as to connect house to barn. Driving along this road, though, we see how the Nutting separation of house and barn becomes an anomaly.

State 121 soon parallels Thompson Lake as it moves toward Oxford, with views of the lake or of lakeside cottages. Again, stone walls line the road until a causeway takes us over the inlet from Greeley Brook near a stately old brick house.

For long stretches on this road, only car and blacktop seem to be of the modern age.

Richard Sherwood, a policy development specialist for the State Planning Office, further defines the nineteenth-century population movements that had such a great impact on how Maine looks today. Just after the American Revolution, he says, the population grew rapidly in Maine, keeping pace with the rest of the nation. But when the Erie Canal opened in 1830, southern New Englanders began heading west for the milder climate and better soils of Ohio, shunning Maine. Growth dropped off so greatly that between 1860 and 1870, Maine actually lost population. Maine has never since officially lost population, but growth has since been slow, booming only slightly during the 1960s and 1970s, when young baby boomers began arriving, frequently as part of the back-to-the-land movement, joined by businesses leaving the cities for inexpensive real estate.

This slow growth aids the image of Maine as a rural, almost antique state, with roads edged by farm and historic farmhouse. But Maine is not a rural state. Only five percent of the workers—at most—have rural occupations, such as farming, fishing, or logging. And only 20 percent of workers even have a connection to the state's natural resources, working in paper mills or canning factories. Trade and service occupations have surpassed manufacturing in Maine's employment base.

Driving down the hill into Oxford, we see a large Greek Revival home on a hill to the left. This is Highfields, maintained in its original condition by descendants of the 1834 builders. The small Victorian structure on the land is a playhouse built in the late nineteenth century.

The Freeland Holmes Library in Oxford can also be worth a stop. This was built from plans by architect Harry D. Olmstead of Hartford, Connecticut, on the site of an old blacksmith shop. The interior has paintings by Harry H. Cochrane, the Renaissance man who designed the wonderful Queen Anne–style complex in Monmouth where the Theater at Monmouth resides.

Here on the banks of Thompson Lake, the town of Oxford, population 3,000, appears to live in an earlier age centered around the Robinson Manufacturing Company, an old woolen mill with a much-visited "mill end" store selling seconds and ends of their woolens as well as other fabrics and notions. The mill stands in a rather weathered and historic enclave of homes.

But as we continue north up State 121, Oxford grows more modern until, at the corner of State 26, we come upon a large mobile-home factory. Turning left onto State 26 north, we pass more mobile- and modular-home plants (there are at least four in this town), as well as the Oxford Speedway, a racetrack for stock cars and a mud run, for a time the largest raceway in New England. We are now hurtling into the late twentieth century.

Across from the speedway is the Oxford Plains Funpark, with go-carts, mini golf, and an arcade—a possible stop for travelers with children.

Wintertime travelers, especially those who may want to rest a little bit longer in the nineteenth century, may turn south on State 26 and go just 200 yards. At the Welchville Inn, David and Anne Carter operate a combination farm and inn from their 1820 cape home. Here, the Carters also maintain cross-country ski trails and rent skis at their ski shop. Perhaps this is the place for a moonlit ski beneath trees glistening with ice.

We, however, remain steeped in the twentieth century as we drive north on State 26 and into Norway, where half a dozen fast-food restaurants immediately scream for our attention.

I've been told that the BarJo Restaurant, at 210 Main Street in Norway, is a special spot for home-cooked meals. Built in 1937 with a sheet metal facade, it was the first Maine restaurant to boast an all-electric kitchen. Not being hungry, I turn right onto State 117 and head into South Paris, where a favorite children's toy store invariably halts me.

Maine has a diminishing number of noncommercial stores for children. The Toy Shop is special for its focus on art and science supplies. I stock up on blank cardboard sheets cut into puzzle shapes for making our own puzzles.

There's a large lake here, and nearby woods, and some exceedingly interesting architecture throughout the towns. But we continue west on State 26, past the Paris Historical Society, stopping for a moment at Snow Falls Gorge, where the Little Androscoggin River leaps down a series of cascades.

After about six miles, beyond the intersection with State 219, we come to Trap Corner and Perham's. This store has everything from stones rough in the rock to jewelry in elaborate gold settings. Perham's also sends people to its own old quarries to dig around in the rocks.

I speak with Dennis Creaser, a young rock hound who explains of himself, "Every kid goes through a dinosaur stage—I just never graduated." From fossils he moved to minerals and then to gems. He and two friends got serious enough to lease some land in Maine's White Mountains above Fryeburg and to get a license allowing him to detonate charges. One day, while "fooling around" there, "looking for just some rocks to put in our collection," he came upon a deposit of amethyst "that just never seemed to end—5,000 pounds the first year, 1,000 pounds the next."

Then the headaches began—worry over poachers, worry over a sudden blossoming of friendships. "It was fun for two weeks, but it lost its attraction real quick," says Creaser. And, no, he says, he's not rich. "But I did get some new toys. I bought myself an ATV."

These deposits are part of a strip extending from Georgetown (see Chapter 5) on the coast through Auburn and Paris Hill to Bethel, continuing into New Hampshire. The deposits developed from volcanic activity some 300 million years ago. Through erosion and rain, some of these gems have come close to the surface, revealing veins of amethyst, topaz, aquamarine, and Maine tourmaline. Perhaps one-third of all the kinds of gemstones in the world can be found in quarries in Oxford County.

Perham's quarries are about five miles west of the store, down State 219 in Greenwood. There's no charge for digging at their quarries. "You can bring what you want to dig with," Creaser says, "sledgehammers, shovels, or screens, but I've seen people go with their bare hands and come up with finds that are better than anything anyone's ever found with tools. Good eyes win over tools, hands down."

We return to South Paris on State 26 (though High Street south from West Paris would make a round-trip route). As we near South Paris, I follow signs for Paris Hill Road.

At first, Paris Hill Road feels like any back road of Maine—a mixture of old homes and new trailers—until we get to the Paris Hill Country Club. Behind the club is a small village without stores where farmers of 150 years ago lived in close contact, their fields spreading downhill from behind their homes. These were wealthy farmers, prominent states-men of an important shire town; their homes are imposing Federal and Greek Revival structures, one seeming more lovely than the next.

Paris Hill retains this glory because of one of history's ironies: it lost its importance. When the railroad came, in 1850, South Paris and not Paris Hill was chosen for the depot. There, in the river valley along the Little Androscoggin River, South Paris grew into a thriving commercial center, eventually siphoning all county offices away from Paris Hill. By 1895, Paris Hill lost its stature as shire town and became simply a residential community.

Paris Hill represents a rural culture in which farmers exercised their minds as well as their backs. Raised here were an unusual number of distinguished men, including four Maine governors, two U.S. senators, twelve U.S. representatives, three speakers of the Maine house, and three presidents of the Maine senate.

But none received greater prominence than Hannibal Hamlin, who served in both houses of Congress, as a Maine governor, as minister to Spain, and as vice president during Abraham Lincoln's first term, from 1860 to 1864. Being a more avid abolitionist than Lincoln, Hamlin was jokingly referred to by the president as his "best insurance against assassination." That may have been true, for it was only months after

Hamlin lost the vice-presidential nomination to Andrew Johnson (vice presidents were nominated independently of presidents at the time) that Lincoln was killed.

Hannibal's birthplace, the Cyrus Hamlin home, was built at the moment when Paris Hill was chosen over Livermore Falls as shire town for the county. It is the most exceptional building in the village. Later owners of the house added a two-story glassed-in porch and a covered walkway that perfectly frames the view westward to the White Mountains.

Today the home is owned by Robert Bahre, past owner of the Oxford Plains Speedway, current owner of a similar enterprise in New Hampshire. His domain also includes a large collection of antique cars, stored in a building behind the library and open to the public during the Paris Hill Founders Day, held yearly on the third weekend in July. And every other year, the historic Paris Hill homes open for a holiday house tour on the first weekend in December.

The neighboring library is public. Librarian Schuyler L. Mott gives tours of the small structure with its crevices of local history.

The library has been fashioned from the old Paris jail. Next door stands the house built for the jailkeeper. He had to be married, says Mott, for the wife was in charge of feeding the prisoners. At least one prisoner, apparently, was quite well fed. According to legend, one night in about the 1830s, four prisoners worked one of the granite blocks loose. Three escaped; the last one was too fat. When the jailor came to work the next day, he found the man stuck like A. A. Milne's Winnie-the-Pooh, caught in a rabbit hole from eating too much honey. All night long, in that 24-by-17-inch opening, the prisoner's face tasted freedom while his legs touched doom.

Though Mott is a man of many stories, when he thinks of his childhood in the 1930s and 1940s, he remembers sounds. He tells me of waking to cowbells every morning as the farmers from the inner circle of the village drove their cows down the road to pasture. Dinnertime was signalled by the return of the bells.

In winter, the cowbells would be joined by sleigh bells as the schoolbus took children up the hill past his house to the neighborhood school. The schoolbus was a large box with benches all around that was placed on a sleigh in winter and rested on a buckboard in spring and fall. Always it was driven by horses.

In addition to politics and architecture, Paris Hill is known for the rock inside Mount Mica. There's full-spectrum tourmaline there, with colors from watermelon to green. According to Dennis Creaser of Perham's, there's a carefully guarded operation mining the gem. Unfortunately, they don't like visitors.

Leaving Paris Hill, we take the Christian Ridge Road toward State 117. Standing with my back to the church, that's the road directly ahead of me. It crosses the old Buckfield Road. Then, after about a mile, there's a blue-gray house with a sign saying Moose Crossing Farm, with sheep in front. I stop to admire the wool that Anne Gass offers, and find that she and her husband, Allen, also run a bed and breakfast in their old New England farmhouse—or farmhouses. This long attached house and barn began with a 1790s cape, to which an early-nineteenth-century cape was added—probably, agrees Anne, by a son or daughter who stayed around to farm the family land and care for aging parents. Anne, who was born in Portland, raised sheep in Washington state for six years before moving back home— with her sheep, sixteen up and sixteen down, in a stock mover. "The sheep did fine," she says. "I was a nervous wreck." Anne spins the yarn, dyes some of it, and knits it when she has time. She demonstrates spinning for her guests.

In summer, or on October weekends, this is a place to stay for visits to the Celebration Barn on the Stockfarm Road, less than a mile down on the right. Here, in a great red barn with its own masklike face, Tony Montanaro has introduced hundreds of students to the sorceries of mime, juggling, puppetry, mask, and dozens of other related techniques. He began with classes and eventually developed a theater company known as the Celebration Mime Theater. Now the place is run by Carol Brett. Come summer, teachers and students still flock from around the country and across the Atlantic for classes in a variety of theater arts. Montanaro returns to teach, along with many a juggler, mime, and other new vaudevillian. Friday and Saturday nights in summer, public performances are also held. Recently, the theater has added Halloween events.

While developing a wide range of classes, Montanaro, an imposing man of dark, masklike features, and Pamela, his former wife, raised eight children in the large farmhouse and surrounding orchards. Though the children have left, many of the students have remained, populating the surrounding hills—and much of the rest of Maine—with a surprising number of practitioners of all sorts of related arts.

We continue on this road to State 117, then turn left. Those itching to stretch their legs may wish to turn right down the Streaked Mountain Road, where a half-mile trail leads up 800 feet to Streaked Mountain, with vistas toward the Oxford hills across rock formations containing mica, quartz, and black tourmaline.

State 117 is a windy, hilly, back road of old orchards and forests, with farm vehicles lumbering along. This is a working road. Traveling in early autumn, the air already fragrant with apples, I find myself wishing for a spare lifetime to spend on a farm here, warmly nestled in these hills.

49

We come now to the small town of Buckfield, with fewer than 1,000 people. Despite the great warehouse of apple crates we pass on our way into town, Buckfield, founded in 1793, seems a quiet place. A hundred years ago, though, Buckfield was a typical small manufacturing village. Mills produced long lumber, shingles, staves, box boards, flour, meal, shovel handles, snow shovels, brushes and brush blocks, hand sleds, powder kegs, leather, and harnesses.

Little of that industry remains. There's a bridge over a waterfall and a library with shingle-style architecture designed by the shingle-style monarch himself, John Calvin Stevens. This Zadoc Long Free Library was the gift of native son John D. Long, governor of Massachusetts, congressman, and secretary of the navy, in memory of his father.

Until recently, Buckfield was also the home of two of Montanaro's prime students, Benny and Denise Reehl, creators of the Buckfield Leather and Lather Show, which they still perform around Maine. They have since moved to Gardiner, on the Kennebec River, and have enlisted a great amount of community support in renovating Johnson Hall, an old opera house, for a school and performance space.

State 117 turns east at Buckfield toward Turner. For five to six miles, we follow a peaceful wooded path wandering near the Nezinscot River, which offers some easy canoeing. Then we turn north onto State 4 in Turner, which takes us toward the Norlands Living History Center, Maine's premier historical village.

We are again on a supply line, a broad, commercial corridor that serves the mill towns of Livermore Falls and Chisholm (see Chapter 4), the college town of Farmington, and the ski areas of the western mountains. There is something quite real in routes like this, though not that ever-touted "real Maine" that is supposed to be the opposite of the "Vacationland Maine" we advertise on our license plates.

People must shop somewhere: in Maine, it's either in small towns such as Norway and South Paris, which have ballooned into regional commercial areas, or on major through routes such as State 4. This road seems to be where people find their "toys." There are used cars for sale, and motorcycles, above-ground pools, and snowmobiles.

Mainers connect deeply to the beauty of Maine, each in his or her own way. There's my friend from a paper-mill family with a hot tub on a back porch that is surrounded by fields and brush. When her son comes home from school, he takes an all-terrain vehicle through the brush to visit his grandmother. And at night—summer and winter—the family reviews their day together, gathered in the hot tub beneath the stars.

When I think of those pools, cycles, and snowmobiles, I no longer think of rampant tinkering with technology. I think of connecting.

The Norlands Living History Center is another way of connecting. It's an active bit of history where people participate in the routines of the previous century. To get there, we bear right onto State 4 and State 108 at Livermore, a town that apparently did not develop appreciably after it lost the battle of the shire towns with Paris Hill. We continue straight on State 108 as State 4 veers off to the north. Among the battered old homes, we watch for signs for the Norlands Living History Center, a left turn before State 108 turns sharply to the right.

At Norlands, farmhouse and barn have been left as they were when a farming family lived and farmed here, serving the Washburns, who lived in an Italianate mansion adjacent to the house. These homes, along with a church, library, one-room schoolhouse, and other buildings, have become a living history museum, where sheep are sheared, water is pumped, and hay is mowed using the technology of a century ago.

A wonderfully enthusiastic women's studies student leads me around the grounds. Every portion of the Washburn-Norland legacy excites her.

Our first stop is the one-room schoolhouse, where I sit at a desk carved by generations of absent-minded students. I attempt to write my name with a quill dipped in ink, but my hand seems no more dexterous than a claw.

We make our way to a library filled with volumes written by the wildly successful Washburn sons, and with portraits of most of the family. Here my guide explains the rags-to-riches story of the Washburns.

The original Washburn homestead was built by Cyrus Hamlin. When Paris Hill became the county seat, Hamlin moved south, selling his home to Israel Washburn, who ran a store that went bankrupt (probably due to the population drain south from the loss of the county seat). Washburn's children grew up in poverty. Nevertheless, each of his seven sons rose to national prominence (we don't hear much about the three daughters). Pushed, some say, by their mother, the family became a Kennedyesque dynasty, the sons making names as congressmen, governors, businessmen and diplomats, a ship's captain, and a newspaper editor. One son was both a governor and founder of the company that was to produce Gold Medal flour.

Then the homestead burned down. Remembering their ancestral farm and the little store that bankrupted their father, the Washburn sons rebuilt the house as a mansion in 1867, visiting there during the summers. After Israel Washburn died, time at the mansion was parceled out to descendants more or less by the week. But 100 years later, fewer and fewer actually returned.

Enter Billy Gammon, a former schoolteacher hired to watch over the place. Gammon grew fascinated by the history encapsulated here. She rounded up the 100 heirs and got them to donate the place to a newly created nonprofit museum.

Today, the center is orchestrated as a journey into the past, mostly to the 1870s, but also to the 1790s, using an older cape on the property. Visitors coming for the weekend are given a character and expected to remain as that person (whether servant or master) for their stay. The focus is so rigorous that college credit can be obtained.

Even though I'm here only for an afternoon, my guide makes sure that I get my hands dirty. Within the many-compartmented barn, we visit the icehouse, where despite the summer heat the ice that had been sawed with great-teethed sawing tools from a nearby lake last winter remains frozen, insulated by sawdust. Then we go to a small corn mill at the edge of a treadmill. Sometimes goats are placed on the mill, sometimes energetic little boys, but this afternoon it is my turn. As I walk—quickly—on this uphill-sloped tread, a primitive version of a jogging track, small teeth turn corn pellets into cornmeal.

Later, we gather eggs from a multicolored hen. My guide slips the eggs into her apron and we return to the kitchen. But as she gallantly holds the door for me, an egg falls from the cupped apron. "What a waste!" we exclaim, both of us suddenly in character and feeling the pinch of one less egg. In the kitchen, we pump water from over a slate sink onto a rag and then return to wipe up the mess.

After my tour of Norlands, I spend a few minutes speaking with the director, Curt Bonney, a native of Livermore Falls, who has since left the museum. He's a quiet, low-keyed man who treats his work with missionary zeal. He wants local children to find pride—and confidence—in the accomplishments of their ancestors.

We speak about the region and about how wars depleted it, especially the Civil War and World War II. Yes, there were fatalities, proportionally more to Maine soldiers than to those of any other state, but also there was wanderlust. Having seen the world, many local boys were reluctant to remain in

*At Norlands you step back in time to help with the haying or cook
for the farmhands on a woodstove*

Maine's backwoods. But, as we've seen, Maine's farm children had been leaving even before the Civil War, and kept leaving afterward—to log in the woods, to work on the railways, to live in the more prosperous valleys to the south, where the railroad brought more business and the mills brought more work.

I drive down the Norlands road to State 108. Century Elms Farms, on the corner, has apple trees where visitors can pick their own Macs from September to mid-October.

Clint Boothby and his brother, Rob, work the farm here, along with their father. These people didn't succumb to wanderlust; the farm has been in the Boothby family for six generations.

"My great-great-grandmother and my great-great-grandfather lived on adjacent farms," says Clint. "They got together and doubled their farms." They also probably combined houses. Clint lives in their farmhouse, an 1820s cape that came from the previous farmers of this land. Like so many farmhouses, the structure streams out to a barn. The original farm was a subsistence operation; a little of everything was produced. Apples came a century later, during the Depression.

"Every generation has tried to be innovative," says Clint, who runs the dairy end of the farm—milking about 120 cows and raising corn and hay for feed. In tough times, they can cut from an extensive woodlot.

Clint says he never planned to be a farmer, but an attorney. In his second year at the University of Maine he switched his major to agriculture. In 1994, Clint attempted to continue another local tradition—that of the statesman farmer. He ran for a seat in the Maine House of Representatives, but lost.

From here, you can follow State 4 south directly to Lewiston-Auburn and the Maine Turnpike. Or, head north on State 4 to its junction with State 17 and catch the tail end of the journey in Chapter 4, along State 17.

In the Area

Pear's Ice Cream, Casco.

Freeland Holmes Library, Oxford, 207-539-4016.

Oxford Mill-End Store, Robinson Manufacturing Company, Oxford, 207-539-4451.

Oxford Plains Speedway, Oxford, in season, 207-539-8865; off-season, 802 244-6963.

Oxford Plains Funpark, Oxford, 207-539-8330.

Welchville Inn, Oxford, 207-539-4848.

BarJo Restaurant, Norway, 207-743-5784.

The Toy Shop, South Paris, 207-743-8697 or 800-293-8697.

Perham's of West Paris, 207-674-2341/-2921/-3530 or 800-371-4367.

Hamlin Memorial Library, Paris Hill, 207-743-2980.

Celebration Mime Theater, Stockfarm Road, Paris Hill, 207-743-8452.

Moose Crossing Farm, Paris Hill, Anne and Allen Gass, 207-743-7656.

Paris Hill Founders Day, Paris Hill, third weekend in July, and Christmas House Tour, Paris Hill, biennially first weekend in December, Judy Loper, 207-743-6226; Mary Alice Bancroft, 207-743-8270.

Lowell Orchard, Buckfield, 207-336-2411.

Maple Crest Farm, Buckfield, 207-336-2466.

Zadoc Long Free Library, Buckfield, 207-336-2171.

Norlands Living History Center, Livermore Falls, 207-897-4366.

Century Elms Farms Inc., Livermore Falls, 207-897-4848.

4 ~

Granite

to Grove

Getting there: Take US 1 up the coast to Rockland.

Highlights: *Route 17 from end to end: Rockland to Rangeley. The Farnsworth Art Museum and Homestead; Fort Western and the Maine State Museum in the state capital; Maine's mill towns; panning for gold; camping at Rangeley Lakes; the Wilhelm Reich Museum; chainsaw wood sculptures; and the history of logging at the Rangeley Lakes Region Logging Museum.*

Traveling around Maine in preparation for this book, I have been thinking a lot about roads. I notice how roads both determine our experience of an area and are determined by a larger collective experience of the need for the road: to get ourselves and our goods from one place to another—from river to river, for instance, or from coast to capital.

Most of the trips in this book twine through Maine in an attempt to find engaging, slow-paced roads. As a result, we frequently shift from one road to another. On this trip, the road is our guide. We take one road only, just to see what happens. I've chosen State 17, from end to end—Rockland to

Rangeley—or more precisely to Oquossoc, some seven miles west of Rangeley.

What do we gain? A cross section of Maine traditions, a trilogy that passes from coastal fishing and quarrying to inland agriculture and industry, ending with lumbering and wilderness recreation in Maine's western mountain woodlands. State 17 begins as one of Maine's essential secondary arteries, leading from the coast to the capital. The second part passes through some of the state's industrial river cities along the Androscoggin. On the final leg, a mountain journey to the Rangeley Lakes, State 17 becomes one of Maine's secret, spectacular beauty spots.

Rockland is easily accessible via US Route 1 up the coast, or by modifing the journey in Chapter 5.

Rockland is a coastal port town, frequently more leathery than lovely. It was named not for its harbor, but for its rock quarries, "the foundation on which the prosperity of the place rests," according to the 1850 petition that netted the city's name change from East Thomaston to Rockland.

The Native American name, however, celebrated the harbor, calling it Catawamkeag, or "great landing place."

Its history weaves rock and harbor—shipbuilding, fishing, fish packing, and quarrying. Though granite was also quarried, limestone was Rockland's most important product; the city was the premier lime producer in the U.S. To turn limestone into cement for construction, it had to be baked in hot kilns. By 1888, there were eighty kilns along the Rockland waterfront, close to their transport ships. Today, lime is still quarried and fired for cement at Dragon Products Co., but now the plant is located near the quarry and near rails and trucking transport, on US 1.

Like most coastal towns, Rockland also built ships, but here the shipping industry flourished from the need to move the lime from Rockland to New York, Virginia, New Orleans, and the West Indies.

Although many ships were built in Rockland, none was more famous than the 1853 clipper *Red Jacket*. It was the largest ship built in Maine to that date, 251 feet long and weighing 2,300 tons. Schools let out to mark her launching on November 2, 1853, when she was towed to New York to be fitted with masts, spars, rigging, and sails. Then she took her maiden voyage, leaving New York for Liverpool, England. Thirteen days, one hour, and twenty-five minutes later, she arrived in Liverpool, "still a record for single-hulled sailing ships," according to Hank and Jan Taft's second edition of *A Cruising Guide to the Maine Coast*. When she got there, Captain Asa Eldridge refused all tugs, and instead backed the huge clipper ship along the pier while the vessel was still under sail.

With its warehouses and brick Main Street lined with a mix of shops and cafes, Rockland seems like Maine's version of Marseilles. Unlike Camden to the north, whose elegant stores prance for the visitor, Rockland is a city that hides its mysteries. It's a city for exploring.

The Shore Village Museum in town has a wealth of lighthouse paraphernalia. Two miles south of town, on State 73, the Owl's Head Transportation Museum is a treat for vehicle lovers, especially for the lucky one who wins the day's raffle of a ride on a slow-moving Waco biplane. At the north end of town, a right turn onto Waldo Avenue leads to the Samoset Resort, adjacent to the Rockland Breakwater, which turns Rockland's "great landing place" into a great mooring place. The breakwater, a mile-long path of granite anchored by a lighthouse, projects directly into the harbor, offering a perspective of Rockland sheltered by the Camden Hills. For a gentler walk, a footpath leads along the waterfront.

But Rockland's greatest treasure may be the William A. Farnsworth Library and Art Museum, with its 6,000-piece collection focusing on American art and the role of Maine art within that larger category. The museum has an ample collection of paintings and drawings by the Wyeth family as well as an extensive collection of the work of Louise Nevelson, about whom you can read more in this chapter.

Renovations in 1994 expanded the Farnsworth and added the Nevelson-Berliawksy Gallery, for the display of twentieth-century art. The expansion also brought an attractive museum shop directly to Rockland's Main Street. The museum is open Monday through Saturday and Sunday afternoons for most of the year; it is closed on Mondays in the winter.

The Farnsworth holdings include two historic houses open to the public, the Farnsworth Homestead adjacent to the museum and the Olson House a short drive away in Cushing. The Olsons were favorite subjects of artist Andrew Wyeth, and his *Christina's World* made their farmhouse familiar to the world. Both properties are open from June through September.

The Farnsworth Museum was a bequest of Lucy Farnsworth, who is described in *Maine: a Guide Downeast*, as "the last of her line, an astute businesswoman with wide real estate holdings who lived in frugal seclusion in the Farnsworth House" until she died in 1935 at age ninety-six. To the surprise of many, her $1.3 million estate was given to the city for a library and an art museum dedicated to her father, who garnered his wealth from the lime trade.

Farnsworth hadn't previously revealed much interest in art, but she did have her standards. Having made up her mind to establish this trust, she made the long journey from Rockland to Boston. According to an unimpeachable source, she arrived unannounced at her chosen bank only to find she needed to use the facilities. Seeing this woman dressed in old-fashioned black, and perhaps looking more like a vagrant than a millionaire, the officers refused her a rest room. She went to the next bank, and the next, until she came upon the

Boston Safe Deposit and Trust Company. Yes, she could use their facilities. From the rest room she marched into the president's office to inform him that she was naming his bank trustee of her will. When she died, determining the extent of her wealth became quite an athletic job: stocks, bonds, cash, and trusts were stuffed in mattresses, hidden behind the third-rate paintings that hung on her walls, and stashed in all sorts of crevices around her home.

One block over from the museum, the Cafe Miranda serves an interesting array of international dishes. The seasonal Caldebeck Gallery, between the two establishments, is always worth a visit.

Rockland was the childhood home of a number of important figures of modern art. Poet Edna St. Vincent Millay, composer Walter Piston, and photographer Kosti Ruohomaa were born here. Sculptor Louise Nevelson was raised in Rockland.

Nevelson probably had the hardest time here. Her family immigrated to Rockland from Russia, but she never felt accepted. In an interview about her adopted town, she was typically forthright:

> We were an immigrant family, foreigners in a
> Daughters of the Revolution town. And I think it must
> have made a great impression on me. I was four and a
> half when we came to Rockland, and that was such a
> WASP country. Now it's better. But think of 1905 when
> you have a name like BER-Li-AWSKY, and you come to
> Maine. Many of the people in Maine were very rich,
> believe it or not. And many of them had very beautiful
> homes. And they needed foreigners like I needed ten
> holes in my head.

But Nevelson's brother lived here, and so she would return. At a retrospective of her work in 1985, she expressed

61

the hope that there would be a place for her work at the Farnsworth. In 1994, thanks to gifts from Nevelson and her sister-in-law, Lillian Berliawsky, the Farnsworth opened a Nevelson gallery featuring her rarely seen formative work, including a loving oil painting of a Rockland hillside, large stars twinkling above.

In summer, schooners and excursion boats ply the waters of Penobscot Bay. A ferry trip from Rockland to North Haven or Vinalhaven is possible at any time of year but is most intimate off-season.

To leave Rockland, we pick up State 17 behind the Dunkin' Donuts. At this time of year, close to Halloween, the Victorian homes decorated with grimacing pumpkins seem like haunted houses lining the way out of town. State 17 launches its journey across the state with a golf course, then Chickawaukie Pond and Dodge Mountain. On the left, there's an old graveyard behind a stone wall, followed by some bold mountain vistas.

After State 17 crosses State 90, Ragged Mountain rises majestically beyond Mirror Lake to the north. There are hiking trails up the mountain and a ski lift at the Camden Snow Bowl ski area, a place teeming with family skiers. One wintry morning we ventured onto the toboggan run here for a laughing, screaming—and very quick—thrill. Access roads can be found on the other side of the mountain.

We soon drive through South Hope, with Union and the jogged turnoff for State 131 (discussed in Chapter 5) just beyond.

On the left, just beyond Union and before the turnoff to State 220 to Washington, is a field kept shorn for model planes. It's marked by little more than a weathervane in the shape of a propeller plane, but on weekends it's a hub of arm-sized planes, along with their handlers. We stop to watch. One man has a biplane, another a blue and orange single-winged prop plane. Two older men are tinkering with their flying machines while another watches.

It's a thrilling, joyous sight to see the planes suddenly take off, then loop through the sky, over and around again, like soaring leaps of the imagination. We watch for half an hour, then continue on our way, passing an Uncle Sam mailbox near the cutoff for Jefferson on State 206.

Farther ahead on State 17 is Elmer's Barn. Leaving the rest of the family to nap in the car, I stop for an immersion of antiques, collectibles, and downright junk. Elmer is the muscled man inside who looks like a miniature of the larger-than-life chainsaw sculpture outside. Despite some prices inflated by notoriety, I can still find bargains.

Soon, a right turn up State 32 leads to the Windsor Fairground. Two fairs are held here—the Windsor Fair, an extensive county fair held during the nine days around Labor Day weekend, and the Common Ground Fair, on the third weekend in September. The latter is an agricultural fair organized by the Maine Organic Farmers and Gardeners Association. Locally, it's referred to as the alternative agricultural fair, or the hippie fair. There are no rides, and no coffee or chocolate sold on the grounds. Not even any white sugar is used. Lemonade is sweetened with honey; ice cream is laden with maple syrup.

Rules aside, the fair is as creative as the lives that make it happen every year, a celebration for native Maine farmers, many of whom trace their trade through many generations, and the 1970s influx of back-to-the-landers. There are animals to pet, craft processes to watch, unusual competitions to behold, such as sheep dogs corralling their sheep and log skidding by massive workhorses; and a wide array of entertainment, including stilt walkers, jugglers, folksingers, and puppeteers. There are also plenty of Maine produce and products for sale displayed at a time when people are beginning to think of holiday presents. But one warning: traffic will jam State 17 on the fair weekend.

On our way again back on State 17, we see signs for Togus on our left. Built in 1866 for Civil War veterans, this was the first National Home for Disabled Volunteer Soldiers in the nation. Horace Beals, a Rockland granite dealer, owned the site and attempted to turn the region into a second Saratoga Springs. He failed; Beals died in the Civil War and his widow sold the estate to the federal government. Today Vietnam veterans populate the facility.

We now pass more Maine folk art—an old red car on top of a post raised to advertise an auto shop. On our right is the headquarters for *Uncle Henry's,* a weekly booklet of ads by people looking to sell or swap goods, the publishers making their money in booklet sales. The publication is sold everywhere in Maine, reflecting the lives and dreams of its people with notices like this one: "Trade: Ten gravesites for one cruising sailboat."

As if to welcome us into Augusta, stately pines canopy the road over the city line. We turn right at the T, still on State 17, following signs for the first of Augusta's two rotaries. We drive three-quarters of the way around and then take Memorial Bridge over the Kennebec River.

As we cross high over the river, I look down at the elegant buildings lining Water Street. To get there, we turn right at the first quarter off the second rotary. We pass the old castlelike post office (a late-nineteenth-century Romanesque Revival structure). Across from the postmodern Key Bank building, built to reflect the best of the street, stands an enchanting Children's Museum, offering a maze of activities, from an authentic Depression-era diner to 1990s computer games. The museum was the dream of Julie O'Brien when her first child was born. It was realized ten years and five children later. The time was not ill spent: the elaborate displays and activities, from architecture to art fabric scraps, came to Augusta almost entirely from community donations. Now, but a few years after its opening, it is ready to expand to a second story.

Farther down the street, a low bridge leads back over the Kennebec to Fort Western, a National Historic Landmark, one of the oldest and best preserved colonial buildings in America. The fort was built in 1754 near the site of the old trading post at Cushnoc, which means "the tide runs no farther up the Kennebec." Here is the head of the tide of the Kennebec, which means "river god"—"Manitou Kennebec." The river, which flows from Moosehead Lake to the Atlantic Ocean, has been one of the region's great arteries for centuries.

Just in front of what is now the Christian Science Reading Room to the south of the fort, the Pilgrim settlers of Massachusetts erected a trading post in 1628. John Alden, of "speak for yourself, John" fame, lived here in 1634. By 1650, the post was sold to a trading company. It remained a profitable spot for fur trading until 1676, when attacks by the French and their Native American allies forced the Europeans to abandon most settlements.

Seeking to secure the area, the colonists returned in the 1750s during the French and Indian Wars. Fort Western would serve as a supply post for Fort Halifax, up the river in Winslow, where boats had to be towed upriver by oxen. After the Treaty of Paris was signed, giving Britain control of most of North America, fort commander James Howard bought Fort Western for his home. Howard entertained Benedict Arnold here during Arnold's happier days—before Arnold struggled through the wilderness in a bungled attempt to invade Quebec during the Revolutionary War, before Arnold swung from hero to traitor.

Later, the fort became a tenement. As the railroad eclipsed the river's importance—though log drives and ice cutting continued—the fort became a house of ill repute.

Recently, the fort has been used for public reenactments of colonial life. Dr. Paul Daiute is an Augusta surgeon who volunteers at the museum and frequently performs the role of Howard during reenactments. A Vietnam veteran, Daiute came back to the United States searching for a way to reconnect with his nation—and found it in the colonial era. He sees these pre-Revolutionary battles, commonly known as the French and Indian Wars but better referred to as the French and British Wars, as both proving ground for the colonies and training ground for the Revolution. "It taught us we could fight and prepared us to enter the Revolution," says Daiute.

The main building here is original; the rest are restorations.

For a different sense of life at this time, look into the recent Pulitzer Prize–winning book by Laurel Thatcher Ulrich, called *A Midwife's Tale: The Life of Martha Ballard Based on Her Diary, 1785-1812.* Ballard was a midwife when the eastern banks of the Kennebec were known as the Fort and the western banks as the Hook (from Bombahook Stream). The book is about women's work: assisting at births, winding shrouds around the dead, and the continuous communal efforts of quiltings and barn raisings. A clear picture emerges of life's fullness and the courage and intelligence with which Ballard negotiated her duties.

We cross back over the bridge and continue up the hill to State Street, where we turn left through the rotary toward the capitol building. Across from the capitol, in a low, modern structure, a cultural complex includes the Maine State Library and Maine State Museum. While I stop to find some books in the library—a resource for all of Maine, with an excellent archive of material—Bill takes Daniel through the museum. When I join them there, they are deep in the wonders of this extraordinary place, one of Maine's cultural treasures. Although not exactly a hands-on museum, this is definitely a sounds-on museum. The noises of industry coupled with the hugeness of some of the exhibits—a great lumbering railroad, a portion of a ship's hull raised from the deep (complete with the model trains boxed for the holidays that went down with the ship), looms that swish back and forth, millstones that grind with water splashing from them, and a recent exhibit devoted to 12,000 years of Native American life—make for real excitement. Maine's history and industry, geology and geography put into perspective the many sights we see on our wanderings.

Leaving the complex, we turn back onto Western Avenue and make a left up the hill. Once a street of elegant homes, this is now a jumble of shopping centers. We stay on Western Avenue past the city limits, where the road becomes State 17/State 11/State 100/US 202.

At Manchester, we leave the main drag, taking a right as we continue to follow State 17. Manchester was the home of Samantha Smith, the little girl who helped melt the cold war with her letter to Yuri Andropov and her subsequent visit to the Soviet Union. In 1985, Samantha and her father died in a plane accident, leaving her mother to carry on her directness. The Samantha Smith Center in Hallowell is a working office that her mother maintains. There's also a memorial to the girl at the Visitor Information Center in Kittery.

Orchards line the road here as we begin our climb toward Readfield. Lakeside Orchards sells a variety of apples at its store and also welcomes visitors wishing to pick their own apples. But most of these old farmhouses now belong to

Augusta-area commuters who either work directly for the state or for the multitude of agencies associated with the state government.

Just before we arrive in Readfield, we pass the long, lovely, and deep Maranacook Lake, one of several such lakes that made central Maine a haven for children's summer camps and family summer cottages. Geologists speculate that in prehistoric times, one large lake covered most of this part of central Maine, including Winthrop, Monmouth, Leeds, Greene, Turner, Readfield, Fayette, Wayne, Mount Vernon, and Livermore.

Readfield was the birthplace of the governor who turned Maine into a dry state long before the rest of the nation went that way. In 1851, Dr. John Hubbard prohibited the sale and manufacture of intoxicating beverages. Just recently, the dry question figured again in Readfield as a local store applied for a liquor license, only to find that many residents still wanted Readfield to be dry.

Soon we are climbing toward Kents Hill. At the top of the hill, we pass the private Kents Hill School, as stunning a setting for a high school as one could imagine. The view north over Torsey Lake is so spectacular, especially now with the fall colors showing, that I fear for my driving. I slow down to look while avoiding students, for whom the road is but a part of their campus. The school was established in 1824 as a private religious secondary school at a time when there were no public secondary schools.

Just beyond the turn where State 17 veers left from State 41, the Kents Hill Orchard lets people come in to pick their own apples on their sixty-three acres. Now we are driving over lovely rolling farm country to Fayette, between Echo Lake and Lovejoy Pond, passing a jolly pumpkin-headed man with floppy feet on the dash of a tractor. Funny and grisly Halloween figures are a great Maine folk art. Beginning with simple cornstalk forms, these figures evolved into fully clothed bodies stuffed with rags. Now, people decorate their lawns with fearsome tableaux, such as ghostly sheets fastened to trees, skeleton bridal couples, and bloodied figures emerging from coffins. In some towns, rivalries spring up for the best scenes.

The road now rolls and climbs to Chisholm, sister city to Livermore Falls, where State 17 curves right at a spot known as Shy Corner. We've now left the lake district and entered one of Maine's mill belts, with its frequent odor of sulfur. The architecture here—close apartments opening onto balconies—is a common structure in Maine's mill towns. A scholar of Franco-America, Yvon A. Labbé of the University of Maine, provides a name for these buildings: four-deckers. He confirms their position in the Franco-American culture. "Houses in Quebec all had front porches, meaning it was all right for people to sit and watch what was going on, something the frugal Yankee didn't allow," Labbé says. When the Quebec French migrated to the states to take up millwork, the four-deckers were used to facilitate the convivial ways of Franco-Americans.

Barely have we taken a breath before we're in Jay, home to an immensely divisive strike at International Paper that was broken, 1980s style, by nonunion workers, most of whom came from out of state. They remain.

The Jay paper mill is one of the newest ones in the state, completed in 1965. Downstream, the Umbagog Paper Company at Livermore Falls is one of the oldest ones. It was opened in 1881 by industrialist Hugh J. Chisholm, the first ground-wood paper mill in the East. Chisholm also owned the Otis paper mill in Livermore (on State 4), which produces newsprint. Seeing the benefits of cooperation among paper mills, in 1898 Chisholm merged some twenty newsprint mills under the name International Paper, then served as president of the company for nearly ten years before becoming chairman of the board.

Leaving town, we notice the Jay Hill Antique Auto Museum, topped by a weathervane in the shape of a car, and the Jay Historical Society at the Holmes-Crafts Homestead, a Federal-style dwelling with hand-hewn timbers. Both have limited summer hours.

One hundred years ago, North Jay received some renown when its quarries were chosen for the granite used for Grant's Tomb. The popular nineteenth-century Maine writer Holman F. Day visited the town in 1893 and described it as "a town of rugged laborers, of gleaming white grain, of chips and clink and clang, of present rip, zip boom!"

State 17 forks left to East Dixfield, where it merges with US 2, a major through road of trees and hills that eventually follows the Androscoggin River to New Hampshire. I am sure there are more quaint roads through this region, but we're staying with this one through all its moods. Between Dixfield and Mexico, it's in a heavy working mood. But this is still Maine, and few areas are fully industrialized. One-third of a mile beyond the stop sign is Hall Farms, on your right, a dairy farm that also produces maple syrup. If you're traveling in early spring, the last week in March or first in April, you can see the sugaring process. Call ahead for a tour.

Dixfield was named for Dr. Elijah Dix, who promised he would endow a library if the town were named for him. He got his wish, but all the town got was a crate of worthless tracts. Dixfield was once a prosperous commercial center for wood turning, where numerous small wooden objects, such as clothespins and dowels, were made. Though there aren't as many factories producing wooden products here as there once were, wood turning is still a local industry.

Across the river in West Peru, the Diamond Match Company factory produced matches and clothespins until it closed in the 1980s.

We enter Mexico now, named in honor of the 1818 Mexican bid for independence. A roadside restaurant and bar, the Mexico Chicken Coop, in the Kersey family for forty-five years and three generations, claims to serve five different luncheon specials for under $5.00. Here, US 2 branches off into Rumford and State 17 meanders through the foothills to the state's western mountains.

Because I have a fascination with industrial towns, I commandeer the car for a brief detour off State 17 to drive through Rumford, beneficiary of Hugh Chisholm's "enlightened paternalism." Following US 2, we turn left over the bridge from Mexico to Rumford and continue up the hill.

In 1882, Rumford was a rural backwater, difficult to reach. But Hugh Chisholm had heard there were spectacular waterfalls here, so he took a horse and sleigh and went exploring. What he found must have been something like the following description from Varney's 1881 *Gazetteer of the State of Maine.*

These falls are in the Androscoggin River in the eastern part of the town and form the grandest cataract in New England. Here the whole volume of the river leaps over abrupt and craggy ledges of granite, dashing the spray far into the air. At present there are three or four pitches at this place, but anciently there must have been a descent of greater magnitude, for large holes peculiar to falls are found high in their rocky banks, far above where the waters have run within the knowledge of man.

*The sturdy duplex houses built for millworkers at Rumford's
Strathglass Park*

Chisholm was sold. He bought the land around Rumford, erected dams on the river to generate power, and created his own power company. He bought the two railroads
that came nearest to Rumford. And he bought woodlands.
These acquisitions assured him of pulp for the raw material,
power for the mill, and transportation for the logs to the mill
and paper from the mill. Then he built the Oxford Mill.

At the stoplight, we follow US 2 as it bears left, then we take the next right, through the large brick arches of Strathglass Park, a section of similar-looking three-story brick and wooden duplex homes. Distressed by the sight of his workers living in sod huts, Chisholm created this park. It includes fifty-one brick and twenty-eight wooden homes for workers, who could rent the homes—if recommended by a foreman.

We cross back over the Androscoggin River to return to State 17 by turning left at the light onto US 2 (Hancock Street), returning over the bridge into Mexico. Then we turn left up State 17.

Other migrants to Rumford were the Polish immigrant tailor Stephen Muskie and his bride of two days, Josephine. Their second child, Edmund, was to become a Maine governor and senator before his doomed bid for the presidency in 1972. Along the way, Edmund S. Muskie also chaired the Senate Subcommittee on Water Pollution, helping to reverse the almost lethal tide of pollution of so many U.S. rivers, the Androscoggin among the worst of them.

By the 1970s, the river had been choking for more than fifty years. Log drives coated the river bottom with bark, resinous sap, and wood. Sawmills added sawdust and bark-covered slabs. From the textile mills around Lewiston came dyes and bleaches as well as wool, cotton fibers, and chemical wastes from raw wool washes. To make matters worse, dams built to control the water flow for mills and log drives left the water stagnant and hot and also took away most of the restorative powers that the aeration of falls would have provided. And, of course, the dams prevented fish migrations. But wastes from the three large paper mills on the river caused the greatest problems, each mill adding as much pollution as if it were a city of 1.5 million people. Already in Muskie's boyhood in the 1920s, the Androscoggin River was too polluted for swimming. By the summer of 1941, warm weather coupled with low waters made the pollution intolerable: fumes literally peeled the paint off houses a mile away from the river. White houses turned black, as did household silver—and then there was the stench.

A public protest arose, forcing some changes. But it wasn't until the Federal Water Pollution Clean-up Act of 1972, spurred by Muskie, that paper mills were forced to clean their wastes and Maine's legendary log drives ended. People still don't swim in the Androscoggin south of the mills, unless they wish to prove a point. But each year the water does get better.

Back on State 17, we now drive north alongside the Swift River past a small, old cemetery and the hamlets of Hale and Frye before winding toward foothills the color of soft heather.

We get the first inkling of the coming glory after a fire-truck mailbox where a turnoff leads to Swift River Falls, on our left. Then, as the road follows the river valley north, the view opens north, south, and west to the mountains.

But we're still in farm country. Here the barns are different again—taller, and unpainted, the wood weathered a rich earthen brown.

At Coos Canyon near Byron (named for the poet), we park the car and cross a wooden bridge as the Swift River cascades beneath us. Here I discover that this canyon, with its sculpted stone formations, is a popular gold-panning spot—but not a place to get rich in. According to Dennis Creaser, our gem expert from Perham's, "You might be able to find as much as an ounce of gold there, but that's only worth about $400—and you could spend your whole life looking for that." People still frequently pan here, or just a bit upriver, but they are collectors or members of gem clubs who do it for fun. It's an experience, a way to identify with stories of the wild west and gold diggers, an insight simultaneously into geology and the economy. During the Depression, however, people camped alongside the riverbanks to make the most of daylight to seek out the gold.

To pan for gold, it helps to have the proper pan, which is larger than a pie pan, with higher sides set at a specific angle. Gem shops (including Perham's) carry the pan.

Panning is based on the fact that gold is heavier than most minerals, so it will sink to the bottom. In a pan you pile dirt that might have gold, then hopefully attempt to float it off. What is gold—a few flakes per panload, perhaps—will have sunk to the bottom of the pan.

Continuing north, State 17 begins to climb, passing the western-sounding Letter E Town, leaving the golden-leaved birch trees behind, coming into evergreens. In the distance, beneath misty mountains, a lake glimmers. As we climb, the land continues to open. Pleasant Mountain and Moody, Brimstone, and Elephant Mountains rise from plains of the softest rust and golden colors. At the lookout, called simply Height of Land, we stop, aching for a moment to ponder these views. The air is cool, light. I turn around, giddy with the view. Below, a ribbon of a road traces the shores of Mooselookmeguntic Lake, the largest of the Rangeley Lakes, the name meaning "moose feeding among big trees." This road is the Bemis Road, I am told, where once a railroad led from Rumford to Bemis. Now neither rail nor town exists.

In Mooselookmeguntic are the islands Toothaker and Students, which were recently donated to the state by the Stephen Phillips Preserve Trust. Behind the trust is Bessie Phillips, an aging woman who has worked for more than twenty years not only to secure the land from private development, but also to restrain public access so that each visitor may have a wilderness experience.

In preserving this land, Phillips, now ailing, is completing a dream begun by her husband. Stephen Phillips was a descendant of the nineteenth-century lumber baron David Pingree. Stephen's work had been to isolate tracts of land from the family inheritance so as to preserve those pieces from development. But he died in 1971, before completing the work. Quietly, Bessie Phillips continued, amassing choice lakefront land, until in 1993 she was able to combine her 7,000 acres with 26,000 acres that a public trust also had been gathering. The parcel presented to the public is more than 33,000 acres of undeveloped land, much of it frontage on the Rangeley Lakes. There are sixty seasonal campsites on the Phillips Preserve, all primitive, requiring visitors to walk—or canoe—to get there.

State 17 descends to lake level. A right turn leads to campgrounds at Rangeley Lake State Park, but we keep going to Oquossoc, an Abenaki word meaning "a blue slender trout." This was once the headquarters of the dogsled postal service. Though the sleds served only 100 people, average cargoes weighed 400 to 500 pounds. There was little place else to shop but through the mails.

This is logging territory, tall-tale territory, sportfishing and hunting territory. On Lower Richardson Lake, beyond Mooselookmeguntic, a floating hotel once operated. Guests could fish from their chamber windows.

Now, coming into Oquossoc we pass Tangwala Psychic Learning & Healing Center with psychic consultant Kaimora.

We've done it! State 17 ends here, after winding its way from shore to mountain, passing Maine's farmland and industries, government offices and fishing holes—a solid cross-section of the state.

Our trip doesn't end, however. First we drive past Oquossoc to Haines Landing, where State 4 ends. It is a funny town, the way outbacks can be. One local store advertises art supplies and computer quartz. Where State 4 ends, at the lake, we are still 2,000 feet above sea level. We stand on the shore, craning to see more, longing for a canoe—which can be rented, we discover, in Rangely.

As we drive south on Bald Mountain Road, paralleling the lake, the importance of the Phillips gift becomes quite clear. Along this part of the eastern shore of Mooselookmeguntic, camps line the lake so closely that a visitor cannot gain access. We pass the trailhead for the hike up Bald Mountain, also part of the new public preserve. The hike, a relatively easy forty-minute journey, does provide views of the lake—and the bold northern and western mountains. This road turns into the Bemis railroad bed, lining the shore. Finally, we can see the lake.

But dusk is coming, so we head back to Oquossoc and drive east toward Rangeley, a few miles down State 16/State 4.

On our way, we take one short detour north at Dodge Pond Road to look at the exterior of the Wilhelm Reich Museum, knowing it's open only in summer. Reich, a great but controversial psychologist, thought he had found life energy—what he called "organon." He sought to study it more, perhaps transmit it through his "orgone box." In 1949, he bought this 200-acre plot as a research institute. But the Food and Drug Administration (FDA) accused him of deceptive advertising. Refusing to reply to a 1954 FDA injunction, Reich was arrested on contempt charges and found guilty in 1956. He died in the Federal Penitentiary at Lewisburg, Pennsylvania, in 1957.

We arrive in Rangeley in hushed twilight, feeling as if the town has already been tucked in for the night. Driving through town, we find the restaurant Doc Grant, a gritty but great-looking spot, advertising itself as midway between the North Pole and the equator, 3,107 miles either way.

We take a room at the Town and Lake Motel, which also offers canoe rentals, and retire to the Red Onion for a home-style meal.

Rangeley is a small town of only 1,063 people that opens upon a vast territory. Throughout its northern woods stand old sporting camps and remnants of logging camps. We spend some of the next day exploring the forests and lakes above Rangeley on a network of logging roads. Driving along the northern rim of the lakes system, we find access to Cup-suptic Lake. But this land we have passed has been clear-cut, leaving but a fringe of trees by the road.

Back in town, across the street from our motel, we find an eight-foot kodiak bear. A man hangs in a nearby tree, chased by another, much smaller bear. These wooden creatures are the work of Rodney Richard, one of a breed of sculptors who can fashion rather subtle figures with a chainsaw. He is considered so expert a carver that he was chosen to attend a Smithsonian Museum festival of traditional artists in Washington.

"I make anything I want to. One guy wanted a great big guy thumbing his nose. As long as I got the idea in my mind, I can make them," explains Richard.

At sixty-five, Richard is retired. "I'm working half-days," he says, "twelve hours a day."

He worked most of his life as a woodsman, starting out when trees were cut with an ax, a crosscut saw, and a buck-saw, and removed from the forest by horse. "I bought my first chainsaw in June 1948," he says. It was one of the first in the area. "I bought a used tractor in '54, then a skidder, then a truck with a loader. Now I've sold it all off and I'm working for someone else . . . But once in a while I take a day off and make some big money in the carving business."

He says he's building this museum to ensure that loggers are remembered. "I wanted to preserve the heritage," says Richard. "Cowboys always got credit for doing everything.

Actually it was the woodsmen who built the country. Cowboys got all the hoopla."

And if you believe Page Helm Jones's description of the old-time logger in his book *Evolution of a Valley: The Androscoggin Story*, the logger is not so different from the cowboy.

> He was a breed of his own and a colorful breed too.
> He was usually single and he might be a younger son
> of a pioneer family who saw no advantage in staying
> at home when there was no prospect for gain or land.
> He might be an Irish immigrant off a boat at Boston
> and lured with an offer of free transportation to the
> big woods by an agent for lumbering interests in
> Portland or Bangor. He could be anyone in the way of
> a rough tough, handyman with an axe from Norway,
> Sweden, or Russia who had no family in America and
> was rugged enough to like the wild, hard life of a
> logger and river man. They were transients, not
> settlers, and many of the early ones would grow
> restless after a "season of lumberin'" on the Penobscot,
> move to the Kennebec for a time and then to the
> Androscoggin and the Connecticut and later to
> Michigan and on westward, ever following the
> dwindling virgin pine. The life was a rough,
> swaggering one.

The Rangeley Lakes Region Logging Museum is located by driving east on State 16 a little more than 1.5 miles out of town. At a yearly festival held the last weekend in July, the old ways flow into the new, with logging competitions, equipment displays that range from the old peaveys to the newest computerized clippers, and the making of bean-hole beans the real way—the beans roasted in deep pits, covered with hot coals, the biscuits baked in reflector ovens.

We return on a loop road that takes us into the back wilderness of State 16 west, through a sliver also of New Hampshire, past some astounding natural rock formations at Grafton Notch State Park, and into Bethel. We could have returned on State 16 northeast to Stratton and down through the Carrabassett Valley. The most direct route back to the Maine Turnpike would be State 4 south.

In the Area

Caldbeck Gallery, Rockland, 207-594-5935.

Farnsworth Art Museum, Rockland, 207-596-6457 or 207-596-6236.

Maine State Ferry Service, Rockland, 207-596-2203.

Owl's Head Transportation Museum, Owls Head, 207-594-4418.

Shore Village Museum, Rockland, 207-594-0311.

Cafe Miranda, Rockland, 207-594-2034.

El Taco Tico, Rockland, 207-594-7568.

Second Read Books and Coffee, Rockland, 207-594-4123.

Camden Snow Bowl, Camden, 207-236-4418 or 207-236-3438.

Elmer's Barn, Coopers Mills, 207-549-7671.

Windsor Fair, Windsor, first week in September.

Common Ground Country Fair, Windsor, third weekend in September, 207-623-5115.

Children's Museum, Augusta, 207-622-2209.

Old Fort Western, Augusta, 207-626-2385.

Maine State Museum, State House Complex, Augusta, 207-287-2301.

Lakeside Orchard, Manchester, pick-your-own apples, 207-622-2479.

Kents Hill Orchard, Kents Hill, pick-your-own-apples, 207-685-3522.

Jay Hill Antique Auto Museum, Jay, 207-645-4330.

Jay Historical Society at Holmes-Craft Homestead, Jay, mid-August event, 207-645-2732.

Hall Farms Maple Products, East Dixfield, 207-645-2862.

The Mexico Chicken Coop, Mexico, 207-364-2710.

Rangeley Lakes Region Logging Museum, Rangeley, festival last weekend in July, 207-864-5594.

Wilhelm Reich Museum, 207-864-3443.

Rev-It-Up Sport Shop, Rangeley, snowmobile rental, 207-864-2452.

Rodney Richard folk carver, Rangley, 207-864-5594.

Town and Lake Motel and Cottages, Rangeley, boat rentals, 207-864-3755.

Country Club Inn, Rangeley, 207-864-3831.

Rangeley Inn, Rangeley, 207-864-3341.

The Red Onion, Rangeley, 207-864-5022.

Stephen Phillips Memorial Preserve Trust campsites, Rangeley, 207-864-2003 or 207-864-3474.

Rangeley Lake State Park, Rangeley, 207-864-3858.

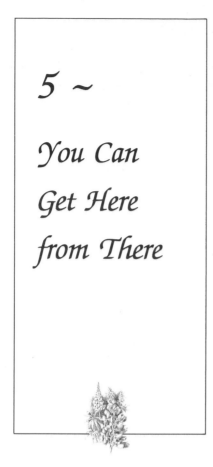

5 ~

You Can Get Here from There

Getting there: From Portland, take I-95 north to Brunswick and exit 22. Take US 1 north to Bath.

Highlights: *The Maine Maritime Museum and Percy & Small Shipyard; Reid State Park's sandy beach; lobster on the wharf at Five Islands; the artistic heritage of Georgetown Island; the antique shops of historic Wiscasset; Boothbay Railway Village; Indian shell heaps on the Damariscotta River; Moody's Diner; WERU's Full Circle Fair; Belfast & Moosehead Lake Railroad; Perry's Moosehead Lake Railroad; Perry's Tropical Nut House; and the Penobscot Marine Museum.*

Most all visitors to Maine eventually find their way up the coast to what people here call down east.

Down east is not a land term but a nautical one. From Boston or Portsmouth, the prevailing summer winds hail from the south or southwest. To get here from there, boats sail downwind, an ideal breeze for moving down the coast, especially a coast that juts out as far east as Maine does. Look at a map. A sailor from Boston to Eastport travels east, downwind.

How to get down east by land?

We could take I-95 all the way, and we do at times. We could also take US 1, but it is long, and jams up a bit.

Here is an alternative we frequently use. It begins along US 1, but where US 1 hugs a bulging coastline, we veer inland and head as due north as the roads allow. Believe it or not, Portland to Belfast by this much more scenic route is barely more than ten minutes longer than I-95. But we're not in this for the speed, so I've snuck in a long detour to Georgetown, a glimpse at Newcastle and Damariscotta, and a visit to Belfast, as well as other stops along the way.

Heading north into Bath on US 1, we pass the marshes that border the New Meadows River, then take the exit for downtown Bath. On this summer day, we wander through the handsome business district, then climb the hill above town on Center Street to Kristina's restaurant. It serves notably tasty dinners, brunches, and lunches, but it is first and foremost a bakery. Today, we're buying treats, choosing between small pastries and chocolate cake slices from the wide array of baked goods in a display case that fronts the restaurant entrance. I remember well the first time we brought Daniel here. We had come for lunch, but after seeing the bakery case, Daniel refused all food. Instead, he pulled a chair up to the dessert case and stared, patiently waiting while we ate.

Our next stop is the Maine Maritime Museum, where exhibits of Maine's salty maritime heritage are set off by the modern structure built with plenty of wood and windows. Outside the building, the Percy & Small Shipyard is the only surviving yard from the days when large wooden craft plied the seas, a good place to ponder the industry that built this coast.

Leaving town, we follow signs for US 1 north, which takes us over the Carleton Bridge, the high drawbridge over

Building a wooden tender at the Bath Marine Museum

the Kennebec River between Bath and Woolwich. I never know where to look on this bridge. There's the road, of course, and the water, but then, down on the right, is Bath Iron Works, one of Maine's major employers, a builder and repairer of naval vessels. While negotiating the bridge, I look for the guns on the destroyers. Number eleven crane looms over the waterfront, like a dinosaur surveying the shipyard. It's the largest crane in the Western Hemisphere, used to lift and assemble the multiton sections of these weighty vessels.

Just over the bridge, for a detour that can last an hour, a day, or a lifetime, we head down State 127, across Arrowsic and over yet another bridge to Georgetown Island.

In the early part of this century, when American artists went about discovering America, these islands were a summer mecca. Sculptor Gaston Lachaise was the first of the group to come here, taking a home farther down on Georgetown Island. Through Lachaise, others came, many connected with Alfred Stieglitz's influential photo-secessionist movement: Paul Strand, Marsden Hartley, John Marin, William and Marguerite Zorach. Most stayed just long enough to paint and photograph the region; the Zorachs bought land in Robinhood and spent long summers in this enclave named for a Native American chief sporting a British underdog's name. Marguerite's work in Maine expanded to murals, and William's to granite sculpture, but the subjects centering both their work were family strength and human dignity. The Portland Museum of Art has a good collection of both Zorachs, including watercolors of the verdant marshes that line this road and sunsets over the coves. Passing these marshes I see a red-winged blackbird, poised on the tip of a reed. Later, I watch a heron and an egret, fishing in the shallows.

A sign from State 127 marks the turnoff for Robinhood on the left. This also leads to a marina and one of Maine's more famous restaurants, The Osprey, named for another summer resident of the cove.

The Zorachs' daughter, artist Dahlov Ipcar, still lives in Robinhood, populating the state with a fantasy array of puzzlelike paintings of animals—colors and designs that began with children's book illustrations and can now be found on the walls of many museums.

Just east of the Georgetown Bridge, at the corner of the Indian Point Road, is the home where Lachaise lived.

Farther down State 127 lies Reid State Park, a beach I prefer in fall and winter, when I can almost have it to myself. The turnoff is marked by an unobtrusive wooden sign and a large, bright American flag painted on a rock.

It is the walks that entice me here, entering along boardwalks crossing spike-grassed marshes and soft dunes. Two beaches totaling 1.5 miles long are broken by boulders and shimmering pools that the ocean leaves behind. After a storm, sand dollars may be strewn across the beaches. "It's a dynamic land," says Ranger John Cooke. "You never know what you will find." One winter afternoon, they almost had to find me, as I nearly got caught on a seabound rock by an incoming tide.

The wood ducks usually leave by November. Wintering over are black ducks, mallards, common mergansers, and such sea ducks as eiders and buffleheads. Loons, too, come to Reid for the winter.

According to Cooke, almost every mammal that lives in Maine can be found passing through Reid—except for black bear. Cooke has seen fox, coyote, raccoon, and porcupine in the park—even moose and mink.

Since this is summertime, though, I head directly to Five Islands, where State 127 ends so abruptly that a car could almost skid off the pier. Houses are built into cliffs that face lower Sheepscot Bay. Porches look out not to the ocean but over the bay, and—yes—to five islands, five rocky islands with evergreens popping out of the stone like angered porcupines. If I were to live in a fishing village, this might be the one.

Each of these islands has a story. Malden Island, off the southern edge of town, where we park, is an island of summer residents with a communal dining hall, so everyone can have a vacation.

But I find it enough to arrive at this village and stare—or eat. The Love Nest Snack Bar, right on the pier, is a busy, businesslike lobster pound and snack bar, serving clam and lobster rolls and fresh boiled lobsters straight from large, steaming cauldrons. While we're picking through a lobster at a picnic table at the edge of the pier, a boat arrives with a new load of victims for the pot. In the distant mist across from us, Hendrick's Head Light warns the mariner of the rocks around Southport Island, where Rachel Carson, author of *Silent Spring*, used to summer. This is maritime Maine; Southport may be just a leap over Sheepscot Bay by water, but getting there by land would take more than an hour.

Returning up State 127, we pass a swimming hole on our right. After the sharp turn at the head of Robinhood Cove, near Lachaise's former home, I look for a tiny house with a Key Lime Pie sign. Robert Verrier, a large man, spends summers in this tiny house. Winter, he migrates to Key West. He bakes his pies here, and creates sculptures, keying a host of miniature items to the pie's lime green. You can find his sculpture at a gallery in Five Islands, but it's more fun to visit him at home. If there's a sign out, it means he's there and selling pies. They're worth a stop.

At the Georgetown Post Office a hand pump offers sweet water to all. Continuing on, we pass some craft stores.

At Georgetown Pottery, visitors can watch potters at their wheels.

Driving back up State 127, I notice the large rock painted like a turtle at the entrance to the Robinhood road. There is another pottery in Arrowsic, before State 127 makes its final curl up to US 1.

Heading north again on US 1, we pass through the commercial section of Woolwich, with several antique and junk shops and the huge Taste of Maine restaurant, frequently sporting a rooftop crab large enough to gobble the entire Georgetown Island. Farther on, car lots alternate with lovely vistas over river and marsh. There are many shopping lures, among them a stand on the west side of the road that sells both gasoline and Mexican pottery in the shape of chickens and angry masked men.

The road curves, then dips toward the Sheepscot River at Wiscasset, where traffic may funnel to a stop at pedestrian walkways. As in many Maine towns, the beauty of the place tells its history. The massive, almost square buildings are of Federal-style architecture, harking back to the young nation's early admiration of Roman styles. Other buildings hail from the colonial era. Wiscasset achieved its fortune as a seafaring and shipbuilding town early in the nation's history; it was the most active port north of Boston. Then came the hostilities that led to the War of 1812, when Britain and France began seizing neutral ships on the high seas. To confront this, Thomas Jefferson issued an embargo act in 1807 and ended all shipping (except up in Eastport, which smuggled goods through Canada, thereby briefly becoming the nation's busiest port—see Chapter 8). Wiscasset never recovered. Once again, the loss suffered by its nineteenth-century population is our gain. Wiscasset holds a wealth of charming, historic architecture, now filled with antique shops and galleries.

There's not much new building here, except for Maine's one nuclear power plant, Maine Yankee. I always think I'm looking at the plant as I peer off the bridge that takes us over the Sheepscot River to Edgecomb, but the brick structure I see is a Central Maine Power generating plant. Maine Yankee, which offered tours until recently, when some students encountered a radiation leak, is hidden down a back road.

I once made the mistake of attempting to pass through Wiscasset on the Fourth of July, while the local parade was crossing US 1. The snake of traffic must have gone on for miles. Wiscasset artist Seaver Leslie painted that scene, though casting it in more apocalyptic terms. Leslie is about as native as a Mainer gets. He works in a converted hayloft adjacent to the cedar-shingled cape his ancestors built in 1739 on the outskirts of Wiscasset. When he was a child, his great-grandmother summoned him to Sunday dinner in one of the classic Federal mansions on US 1. I can imagine her, surely a Victorian, instilling in future generations the virtues of discipline, hard work, and achievement that she learned as one of Maine's class of highly literate nineteenth-century farmers.

In Leslie's painting, it's not the parade that halts the traffic, but two naked men grunting under the weight of the huge log they're dragging across the road, pitting the old ways against the new, righting the balance.

Wiscasset is also famous for the two hulks of schooners in the Sheepscot River that look as if they, too, were from the Victorian era. But the *Hesper* and *Luther Little* were launched in 1918. The final plan for these vessels was to bring freight to the coast by rail and then ship it off by sail, but the schooners' era had truly ended. Mainers have been watching the ships' demise since the 1930s.

The rail, though, did operate, at least from 1894 to 1933, but never very profitably. The Wiscasset, Waterville and Farmington narrow-gauge railroad (which never made it to Farmington) brought children from up the Sheepscot River to school in Wiscasset, as well as milk to a creamery here. Potatoes, corn, and apples were also shipped from inland farms to markets farther south. Though the rail was an essential artery, it was not reliable and had some notorious accidents. Some knew the train by its freight, calling it the "milky way." Others knew it by its reputation, calling it the "Weak, Weary and Feeble."

A few of these cars were later bought by the Edaville Railroad in Massachusetts to take visitors around the cranberry bogs. These same trains may come north again, as part of a narrow-gauge rail around Portland.

After the bridge over the Sheepscot, US 1 climbs a long hill. Before the crest, State 27 on the right leads to Boothbay Harbor, a summer town packed with visitors and stores. On the way, the Boothbay Railway Village offers a miniature railroad trip and a wealth of information on the narrow gauge.

Two miles north of the Muddy Rudder, a left turn at the crossroads leads to an alpaca farm—Cunningham Island Alpaca Stud Farm. Go .7 mile, then take a right onto a dirt road and continue for 1.5 miles. Lucy Harrington has bred animals all her life, but she's fallen in love with her alpacas. They are as different from llamas, she insists, as llamas are from camels. Alpacas are smaller, gentler, sweeter, more adorable, and the fleece is more valuable," says Lucy. "They have these adorable, huge, luminous dark eyes and long eyelashes; they are always inquisitive, always poking around, fun to watch, and very peaceful. Once, I lay down and fell asleep in the pasture. When I awoke, the alpaca were sleeping all around me."

Lucy welcomes visitors; and though she doesn't usually fall asleep on the job, she prefers a call in advance. At the farm, yarn and goods made from the silky soft fleece are for sale.

Just before US 1 crosses the Damariscotta River, US 1B detours into the twin towns of Newcastle and Damariscotta. Below US 1, along the shores of Glidden Point near where Newcastle reaches into the Damariscotta River, lie heaps of oyster shells, the ancient wastes of passing Native Americans living 3,000 years ago.

We might be able to see the middens from the highway, but stopping is dangerous and strongly discouraged. Instead, we take a three-mile round-trip trail leading to these shell-lined banks and alongside the Great Salt Bay. To get there, follow the business route (US 1B) into Newcastle for about a quarter mile, then take State 215 north toward Damariscotta Mills. A little more than a half mile from here, past the post office, is the office of the *Lincoln County News*. A small sign posted across the street marks the trailhead. The shells are toward the apex of the trail, but the entire path is a good bird-watching spot. Osprey nest over the shores of the bay; eagles nest nearby and can sometimes be seen overhead. In winter, when other spots freeze up, hooded mergansers and common goldeneyes may be seen here. Fall and spring migrations are also a good time to see birds. Peter Knauss of the Damariscotta River Association reminds me that much of this trail, including the middens, is on private land; we must tread respectfully.

There are a lot of shells here: more than a million cubic feet of oyster shells, up to thirty feet deep. Shells from a spot known as the Whaleback Midden here were actually harvested a century ago and sent to Boston for chicken feed and gravel. Native American artifacts found among them still lie in the basement of the Peabody Museum at Harvard. Knauss says the Damariscotta River Association has just acquired a saltwater farm nearby and hopes eventually to create a heritage center that may include some of the Peabody material.

But there is no longer a rich source of oysters here. As the sea level rose, perhaps a thousand years ago, the salinity level also rose. That, plus a worm, caused the demise of the oysters. The Native American tribes encountered by the European settlers (a different people from the oyster-eating tribes) feasted on clams.

Newcastle and Damariscotta are quintessential summer towns, their white porches and railings set off by purple, blue, and pink flowers dangling over window boxes. Children's book author Barbara Cooney lives here, behind a garden of lupines. In summer, there are plenty of antique and gift shops in town, and a share of traffic congestion.

Almost at the end of US 1B we come to Round Top Center for the Arts, housed in a large, old farmhouse. Next door is Round Top Ice Cream. The ice cream alone would be cause for a stop, but so is the arts center. A maze of rooms reveals the activities: a substantial gallery, easels for oil painting, looms for weaving. Somewhere in the building a clarinet plays. A barn below the center has recently been renovated for a theater and additional gallery space.

We head back to US 1, where a sign announces the town of Nobleboro. Just over this hill, on a rise over the west side of US 1, stands the cheery Gallery House at Nobleboro, sharing quarters with the Holly Hill Nursery owned by the husband of gallery director Marcia Stewart. The gallery is small, inviting, and frequently filled with art that casts a personal light on Maine rural existence.

"Down" the coast, Waldoboro follows Nobleboro. There's a business section on US 1, but the heart of town—with its authentic five-and-ten store, cafe bookstore, classic theater, and several galleries—lies south of the highway.

Shortly beyond the turnoffs for Waldoboro we come to Moody's Diner, Maine's most famous diner. The food here is fresh and seasonal, and though the meat is no longer grown

on the premises, much of it, along with the vegetables, is still
bought locally. Eating at Moody's is something like eating at a
town's chicken barbecue. Despite its fame, Moody's has managed to keep a local atmosphere. So it was big news when
Moody's recently banned cigarette smoking.

Local food, no smoking—these sound like the standards
a gourmet or organic restaurant might keep to. But Moody's is
very much the down-home Maine diner serving such specials
as New England boiled dinner and corn chowder. Perhaps
Moody's is simply an example of how modern it is to be
behind the times. Newer restaurants may be only recalling an
age that Moody's has yet to leave.

Eight-tenths of a mile beyond Moody's, we turn inland
on State 235. What inspires me here is the contrast. US 1 is
continually aware of its travelers. Now we're on the quiet
roads, back roads that guide people to their homes or to their
recreation—to lakes, perhaps, or a dance hall. So this road
reveals the way much of Maine lives, which is not in towns
but spread along the countryside, in big houses and little, in
patched-up trailers and beside large gardens. Frequently in
Maine, the road is the town.

On the east side of the road stands an old red house with
a boat weathervane and a sign advertising Winks Bottle Shop.
The walls of the store are lined with bottles, but it is the name
that attracts me. I imagine winking bottles and am satisfied.

Opposite is a small Christmas tree farm. Then the road
meanders along a succession of Maine vistas: a grove of tall
pines, some deep woods, trailers and suburban homes, fields
of cabbages, and then a pocket cemetery at a peninsula of land
between State 235 and Western Road. There's a stop sign here,
and the road bends sharply, overlooking Seven Tree Pond.
Soon we drive along the pond, though forests and higher
fields sometimes obscure the view. We come to fields on both
sides of the road, then to a boat launch. In spring, we could

easily take a small boat under the bridge to Round Pond, paddling beside otter and beaver as far as Union's fairgrounds before rapids on the Saint George River would make it too difficult. Indeed, we could paddle south to tidal waters from this chain of ponds and the Saint George River, if we wanted.

Entering Union by road, though, it is architecture more than nature that I notice. This is a town filled with Victorian details, such as filigree carvings on structural supports. With a population of 1,989, Union is as large as Damariscotta or Newcastle, but it appears more rural, the difference being the seasonal traffic of the coast. Union is a stately town, built around a large green common. We drive around the gazebo-studded green, following the road that snakes to the left of the common, near the cafe and gift shop. We cross the Saint George River, passing near the Union Fairground and Matthews Museum.

The fairground hosts two fairs and a giant antiques show and sale. The WERU Full Circle Fair begins the summer in early July, the Maine Antiques Festival spreads over the grounds in mid-August, and the Union Fair ends the summer the last weekend in August. Between times, Matthews Museum displays farm implements.

Union was named for the spirit of harmony that prevailed in 1786, a mood that continues with the WERU fair, which celebrates eastern Maine's alternative radio station (see Chapter 7). The highlight here is the drumming circle, where hundreds gather, old and young, to bang on anything from imported African drums to kitchen saucepans carried from home.

The Union Fair is as different from the Full Circle Fair as an old general store is from a natural foods co-op. There are sugary treats at the Union Fair, as well as rides, balanced by agricultural booths. It's a good size, too, not so overwhelming that I leave feeling I have missed something. I went there last year with Daniel after a long working day. We indulged in rides and looked at the oversized vegetables, but my main memory is of lingering together at twilight facing a dusky pink in the distance, with hot dogs and sodas on our laps and a kindly old gentleman beside us. I remember him with a cane, sporting plantation whites.

Between the fairs, on the second full weekend in August, more than 350 antiques dealers from all over the country set up shop at the fairgrounds for the Maine Antiques Festival, billed as the largest show of its kind in New England. Buyers and browsers lose track of the hour here, as they travel back in time along the show's grassy aisles. The show's organizers sponsor two more antiques events in Maine each summer, in Bar Harbor and Damariscotta.

At Union, we jog left onto State 17 for a moment, then turn quickly right onto State 131 north, a similarly lovely, winding road. Here, after passing a large warehouse for a vending machine company and a small Christmas tree farm, we come upon several homes with lush gardens. "I want that garden," I say to Daniel. He replies with unaccountable reassurance, "We have the prettiest garden of all, Mommy." It is so overgrown, visitors to our home can't even find it.

The road soon bends toward a small park with picnic tables at the Sennebec Lake boat launch area. It then rises above the lake, affording a spectacular view of the lake and hills beyond.

The Sennebec campground occupies some of the lake here, offering dances on summer weekends. After the lake, we pass a bright sign for the Appleton Village School, complete with an apple, as if the town were fully focused on schooling. Now we pass some forest, then deep woods, and a tall, new gray house with an impressive garden.

The crossroads that is Appleton Village hugs the road. Just beyond, there's a view east over to the next hill, and a white barn selling antiques.

State 105 would take us to Camden along a back way, past Megunticook Lake, if we wanted. But we stay on State 131, passing a farm selling rhododendrons, then another enviable garden and more hills, and a lumber mill, into Searsmont. We stop for a moment at the Fraternity Village Store Cafe, an unusually pleasant place carrying staples and natural foods, offering lunch in an airy room. Sometimes, the walls are hung with local exhibits. Searsmont's nickname of Fraternity comes from the name for the town novelist Ben Ames Williams used. Ames was a popular early twentieth-century author who summered here until his death in 1953.

After a local sawmill known for doing custom work, the road ends as it began, with crowded yards in front of small trailers. Seeing a cardboard sign taped to a mailbox advertising "Free Kittens," we take a look. The yard is filled with items that may yet again have a use—an old washing machine, engine parts, a rusted car chassis. There are chickens in one fenced-off portion, a small garden elsewhere. But the trailer is cramped and overrun by cats. These are people trying to make a Maine living the Maine way, working independently, doing what they can. When houses are small, yards become real adjuncts of the home, just like the dooryards of the old connected Maine farms, where tools were repaired, cabinets built, and jobs finished. The kittens are mere balls of color, too young to leave their mother, so we continue onward.

At State 3 we turn right and head east toward Belfast. We climb a high hill and suddenly Penobscot Bay opens before us, a broad stretch of water embracing islands. We soon meet

US 1 again, a left turn at the bridge on the edge of Belfast, but we stay straight, heading downtown for a moment.

Belfast is an old shipping town with a proud main street that is only now recovering from the loss of the poultry and fish-packing industries that devastated the town like a one-two punch. Since then, there has been an influx of new populations, back-to-the-landers, artists, and elements of Maine's alternative community who live in the surrounding hills and farms, or have come directly to Belfast, attracted by the brick facades on Main Street and the wealth of old homes around town. A fish-packing plant has also opened up.

As we come to town, a large mural of a row of cans on a building on the south side of the road symbolizes both tensions and aspirations: Belfast may once have preserved fish in cans; now it preserves its past, its traditions, its beauty.

We head for a snack at the Belfast Cooperative by turning right at the light in town. The co-op has recently expanded into an abandoned pharmacy, transforming the impersonal, cavernous building into a spacious, wood-paneled grocery, pharmacy, restaurant, and playground, the latter provided by a magic castle complete with toys and a slide. Like an old country store, the new co-op has immediately become the center of the new "alternative" and artists' community. The meeting place for the old guard is Darre's, a breakfast and lunch spot on Lower Main Street, painted with murals inside.

At the co-op, I pass up spicy noodles and settle for a coffee. Daniel gets a muffin, both of us saving room for some of the world's best ice cream.

Cranberry Tiger ice cream is even better and richer than my favorite commercial brand, Ben & Jerry's. And currently it's available only here, in Belfast, at the co-op. Daniel gets the butteriest buttercrunch I've ever tasted; I wait for leftovers.

Happy with our ice creams, we walk to the harbor to wander along railroad tracks searching for treasures. We find

The marvelous old bank building in Belfast

old rusted bolts, a key, and several rocks, which become nesting birds in a cage locked by the key. I keep the bolt.

The tracks here are maintained by the Belfast & Moosehead Lake Railroad, a local excursion company that runs two-and-a-half-hour trips, complete with a mock robbery, west to Brooks and back. The railroad now shares its station with the Belfast Maskers, a local theater group.

Back up Main Street, I peek in the window of the J. S. Ames Gallery, a haven for some fine, sophisticated art, and then at Artfellows, where the artists have reached out to Belfast youths, asking them to make art in reaction to a curfew imposed on teenagers last summer.

We pile into the car now and turn north at the traffic light onto High Street. Until the shopping center was installed up the road near US 1, this light in Belfast was the only traffic light in Waldo County.

Almost at the end of High Street, in a large sea captain's mansion overlooking the harbor, is the Frick Gallery. Owner Rosemary Frick has a good eye for art and the will to exhibit inventive, adventurous pieces. She also has a guest house.

Soon after the Frick, a sign leads us off High Street back onto US 1/State 3 north over the bridge crossing the tongue-twisting Passagassawakeag River (PaSAgasawakag), meaning "sturgeon's place" or "place for spearing sturgeon by torch-light." Locals avoid pronouncing the name, fondly calling it the "Passy."

"Where's the pink dinosaur?" I ask my son. "Where's the elephant?"

The pink stegosaurus skeleton, close to the bridge, marks a gem store. An iguana lives inside. The elephants, farther ahead, signal Perry's Tropical Nut House, a true relic of the roads. Generations of travelers would mark their arrival down east by Perry's treasure trove of musty stuffed animals that share space with candy, nuts, and gifts.

Just after the sea captain sign with his yellow rain gear is a sign for Young's at the harbor of East Belfast. This is another lobster pound, for those who regret turning down the one at Five Islands. As in Five Islands, boats come right to the pier to unload their lobsters. But Young's season extends to fall and spring, serving lobsters in a large warehouse-like building on the pier that once housed lobster holding tanks. The view of Belfast across the harbor is incomparable.

Looking out over Penobscot Bay, I see two schooners like great white angel wings on the horizon. But it is a stretch of the imagination to think of quiet Searsport clanking with hammers and shouts of shipbuilders as numerous ships were built and launched.

A hundred or so years ago, Searsport, Belfast, and Stockton Springs virtually turned their backs to the land, scorning road dust for vessels like the ones now in Searsport harbor. These were oceangoing towns. Searsport sent out more sea captains than any other town in America. One-tenth of the male residents of the town were sea captains; many more Searsport citizens shipped out with them. Even those who farmed the land knew the rocking of the waves, retiring to terra firma only in their middle years. These sailor-farmers lived out their lives spinning yarns of Hong Kong and the West Indies, with Oriental treasures to back up their tales.

Indeed, in 1880 when George Varney came to Searsport to research his *Gazetteer of the State of Maine*, he thought of nothing else:

> The social tourist will often be surprised to find the
> farmer with whom he stops to chat indulging in
> reminiscences of far-off regions, of hurricanes in the
> western tropics, and of cyclones off the Asiatic coast,
> and other strange and thrilling experiences of port and
> sea. Such incidents bring out the fact that among the

independent yeomen of the town are many whose
early years were spent upon the sea, and some who
acquired handsome properties in maritime pursuits.
Often their houses will be found adorned with natural
and manufactured articles of strange beauty from many
climes; while about the grounds, as well as buildings,
is the neatness born of the pride of the seaman in the
trim appearance of his ship.

The bounty of this maritime heritage remains in the elegant homes spread along US 1/State 3 from Belfast to Stockton
Springs, each an architectural gem. But whereas the midcoast
towns we passed through earlier—Wiscasset, Newcastle,
Damariscotta, and Waldoboro—still seem to walk within their
proud past, Searsport is struggling to remember it. The ship
captains frequently moved to Boston or New York once the
money was gone from shipbuilding. Their descendants may
have held onto the homes for a while, but by the 1940s probably no Searsport or Stockton Springs mansion remained in
the family of its builder. The people who remained in Searsport—descendants of sailors, shipbuilders, and craftsmen—
as well as a host of transients from around Maine have
watched as each mansion has been converted to an inn or
antique store, or both.

There is some tension here between native and tourist or
native and persons from away. There is also some rebellion.
Contemporary poet Stephen Dobyns captures the feeling in
the surprising, surreal poem called "Dancing in Vacationland." It begins:

The people in the houses behind Searsport are dancing:
the people in tin and tar paper mobile homes, people
in plywood shacks surrounded by junked cars and
     tires,
broken furniture, hungry geese and chickens, bored

hunting dogs. In ones and twos, they open their doors, weaving and bobbing out to the road . . .

Thinking of past and present, I visit the Penobscot Marine Museum in Searsport. This small museum, created on a street of old homes, safeguards the region's maritime heritage. There are naval battle displays, artifacts from the China trade, and astounding lists of the skilled trades that were needed to build the wooden ships. I feel, yet again, as if I've made a new discovery. The museum also holds a precious stock of marine paintings, including a sequence of paintings detailing the progress of the 1813 battle between the *Enterprise* and the *Boxer*, almost like filmstrips from an animated movie. There are models of large ships and many real-life examples of small ones and a detailed description of the evolution of the sailing vessel—cutters, downeasters, schooners, and the like. Most startling are old photographs showing children with their pets crawling around the decks and rows of men, high above the sea, arranging sails. Through the photos, legends of the sea grow real.

Leaving town, we pass the Homeport Inn, then Hamilton Marine, reminding me that this is still maritime territory.

On the left side of the road at the north edge of Searsport, Sarah Nickerson hooks rugs at her store, the Rug Rat. Her work turns local scenes such as Stockton Springs' main street, complete with its Exxon station, and her own memories of blueberry raking and holiday wreath making into small textile art pieces.

If Searsport is striving to remember its heritage, Stockton Springs is struggling simply to glimpse it. The commercial sector of town has pretty much collapsed since it was bypassed by US 1. The restaurant Just Barb's marks the entrance to Stockton Springs. When I detour here, I see a town that has lost its center, left with only a used-goods harware store, town office, gas station, sub shop, and post office. But driving down any of the roads going into town, I find glorious farmhouses whose breezy meadows lead to the shore. It's like a land out of time. There are a few bed and breakfasts here, too, including the Whistle Stop near some train tracks at the edge of farm and ocean. The church on Church Street has a lovely trompe l'oeil altar, which caused a stir when first discovered. Past the post office, a sign leads us to Fort Point State Park, a gentle shorefront park with a lighthouse, glorious views, and giant earthworks—the remains of the old fort.

Back on US 1/State 3, a few miles beyond town, stands Perry's—Stockton Springs' Perry's—where the animals may be stuffed but they are not dead. I refer to Rosebud the Pig, a thousand-pound pet who lives behind the gas station and convenience store in her own home with roses painted on the door. Rosebud used to forage out in the mud, but these days she doesn't do much but wallow in her little home. She's just too big. To keep Rosebud company, Ed Perry has added a menagerie. There's a rather fierce goat, as well as rabbits, chickens, turkeys, and other less familiar looking fowl. Perry's now sells T-shirts of Rosebud, which the Belfast Cooperative has picked up.

Above Stockton Springs, Penobscot Bay becomes the Penobscot River. At Sandy Point, a small beach has recently become public land. The state put a parking lot here and defined it with huge boulders, but the only indication of its existence is a hint on the sign for the Rocky Ridge Motel on US 1/State 3. Unmarked public beaches are not unusual in Maine. It keeps some places local. The Sandy Point Beach is a right turn off US 1/State 3 across from the motel. Even in midsummer it is frequently deserted, except for the cormorants and osprey who make their home on the abandoned pilings of a fish factory. I've been told this is a good spot for windsurfing.

Leaving the beach, we bypass US 1 for a moment by turning north on a dirt road beside the train tracks. This road takes us past a row of summer homes, now mostly converted for year-round use, leading to the enclave of Sandy Point, yet another village forgotten by time. There are large farmhouses here and, to the right as we come to the first crossroads, a row of smaller homes on Perkins Mill Road. Here lives Caro Hutchins, in the house she and her first husband built in 1924, soon after they were married.

The house next door, ever in her view, is the one in which she was born in 1899. A nephew lives there today. One hundred years ago, Caro's mother was a commuter from the village of Penobscot, along with a boatload of other women who crossed the river to work in a knitting mill in town. But Caro remained in Sandy Point, falling in love with Lindsay Perkins, a worker on a Penobscot River towboat, settling down to raise ten children.

Caro can remember boats towing a string of four, possibly even five sailing vessels up the river. She also can remember the passenger steamers that used to go by on their way from Boston, Rockland, and Belfast, terminating in Bangor.

"I always ran to the window to see the boats passing by," she says. "Still do."

This enclave seems sleepy now, but when Caro was a girl she could hop a train at the Sandy Point station and take it to Winterport, where she worked as a telegraph operator. The settlement also had its own seven-piece band, with Caro on the saxophone. Sometimes the band traveled to Stockton Springs and Searsport to play for dances, but mostly it played right in Sandy Point, at the community hall on the hill.

We continue through town, passing the Sandy Point Post Office, a small room in a large home of the elderly postmistress, who still tends a luscious perennial garden. We meet US 1/State 3 on the other side of Sandy Point. The vistas here are a mix of cliff and sky before the road turns close to the river again. A tugboat blasts its horn as it pushes a tanker to Bucksport. Is Caro at her window?

We are ready to cross the Waldo-Hancock Bridge. This journey can now link with several: the one in Chapter 6, snaking across State 139 and north toward Greenville; the journey in Chapter 7, to Castine, Blue Hill, and Deer Isle; or the journey in Chapter 8, to Eastport.

In the Area

Chocolate Church Art Center, Bath, 207-442-8455 or 207-442-8627.

Maine Maritime Museum, Bath, 207-443-1316 or 207-443-6381.

Kristina's restaurant, Bath, 207-442-8577.

The Osprey, Robinhood, 207-371-2530.

Georgetown Pottery, Georgetown, 207-371-2801.

Reid State Park, Georgetown, 207-371-2303.

Robert Verrier Gallery, Georgetown, 207-371-2781.

Grey Havens Inn, Georgetown, 207-371-2616.

Love Nest Snack Bar, Five Islands.

Nickels-Sortwell House, Wiscasset, 207-617-227-3956.

Castle Tucker, Wiscasset, 207-882-7364.

Boothbay Railway Village, Boothbay, 207-633-4727.

Cunningham Island Alpaca Stud Farm, North Edgecomb, 207-882-7626.

Damariscotta River Association, Damariscotta, 207-563-2196.

Round Top Center for the Arts, Damariscotta, 207-563-1507.

Round Top Ice Cream, Damariscotta, 207-563-5307.

Gallery House at Nobleboro, Nobleboro, 207-563-8598.

Waldoboro 5 and 10 Cent Store, Waldoboro, 207-832-4624.

Le Va-tout B&B Gallery & Gardens, Waldoboro, 207-832-4552.

Waldo Theater, Waldoboro, 207-832-6060.

Bill's Cafe and Bookstore, Waldoboro, 207-832-4613 or 800-696-4613.

Moody's Diner and Cottages, Waldoboro, 207-832-7785 (diner); 207-832-5362 (motel).

Sennebec Lake Campground, Appleton, 207-785-4250.

Union Fair, last week in August, Union, 207-785-3281.

WERU Full Circle Fair, second weekend in July, Union, 207-563-1013.

Maine Antiques Festival, second weekend in August, Union, 207-563-1013.

Matthew's Museum, Union.

Fraternity Village Store Cafe, Searsmont, 207-342-5866.

J. S. Ames Gallery, Belfast, 207-338-1558.

Artfellows, Belfast, 207-338-5776.

Belfast & Moosehead Lake Railroad, Belfast, 207-338-2330.

Belfast Maskers, Belfast, 207-338-9668.

Frick Gallery, Belfast, 207-338-3671.

Perry's Tropical Nut House, Belfast, 207-338-1630.

Belfast Cooperative, Belfast, 207-338-2532.

Bell The Cat Coffeehouse, Belfast, 207-338-2084.

Darre's, Belfast, 207-338-1884.

90 Main Street, Belfast, 207-338-1106.

Young's Lobster Pound, Belfast, 207-338-1160.

Frick Gallery Guest House, Belfast, 207-338-3934.

Hamilton Marine, Searsport, 207-548-6302.

Penobscot Marine Museum, Searsport, 207-548-2529.

Rug Rat, Searsport, 207-548-6093.

Nickerson Tavern, Searsport, 207-548-2220.

Homeport Inn, Searsport, 207-548-2259.

Perry's, Stockton Springs, 207-567-3392.

Just Barb's, Stockton Springs, 207-567-3886.

Hitchborn Inn, Stockton Springs, 207-567-4183.

Whistlestop Inn, Stockton Springs, 207-567-3726.

Sail Inn, Prospect, 207-469-3850.

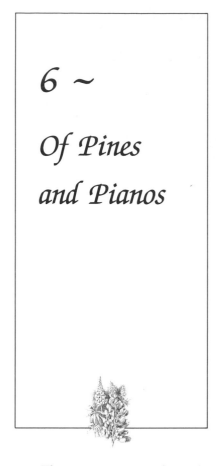

6 ~

Of Pines
and Pianos

Getting there: From southern Maine, take I-95 to Augusta, then take State 3 to Belfast and US1/State 3 north to Bucksport.

Highlights: *Fort Knox; historic towns along the Penobscot River; the Bryant Stove Works and Museum (with antique cars, a calliope, and eight nickelodeons); a trip through farm country and mill towns; a visit to one man's enchanted forest; hiking on Boarstone Mountain; and fishing in Lake Onawa.*

This is a journey through inland Maine, through the rolling hills where Maine's all-purpose farmer still lives. Beginning in Bucksport, we travel to Fort Knox and up the Penobscot River to Winterport, across central Maine and north near Dover-Foxcroft, and then to the wilderness around Onawa, just below Greenville. These are Maine's quiet hamlets, the image of rural farms. And from Onawa, it's only a short trip to Greenville at the edge of Moosehead Lake.

It is late November and I am traveling with my whole family—Bill and Daniel—in our red 1977 Chevy pickup with a camper-top humped on back. We begin in Bucksport, a small mill town on the Penobscot River. To get there from southern Maine, either take I-95 to Augusta and cross State 3 to US 1/State 3 north, or take I-95 to Bangor and exit onto I-395 to State 15 south toward Bucksport.

We begin with morning coffee at the Dockside Restaurant in Bucksport, where locals come to eat breakfast in front of one of the best views in town—over the Penobscot River as it widens around Prospect on its way toward Bangor. How many Maine towns—even tourist ones—can boast such a view with breakfast?

This morning, the first snow of the year has fallen, a light snow, enough to cast an air of enchantment on the embankments of Fort Knox, across the river, but not enough to deter us from our aim of a hike and canoe trip on Lake Onawa.

The window puts Bucksport in perspective. North on the river is the Champion paper mill, spewing smoke thick and white in the cold. The mill is by far the largest employer here, operating round the clock with otherworldly lights. Were it summer, we could take a tour of the papermaking process. Earplugs are mandatory and provided by the management.

Fort Knox is across the river, an emblem of gentleness, bathed in white flakes. Below us are the docks. Large tankers come here frequently, bringing light petroleum products like fuel oil and diesel gas that will be transported throughout northern Maine, to Bangor, Eastport, Rumford, even Fort Kent. Tankers and barges alike are pushed upstream by bright-red tugboats. When the crew gets a break, Bucksport becomes an international port, where exotic faces and unusual accents flow through, trying to decipher the American supermarket. Bill Carpenter's poem "The Ecuadorian Sailors," about foreign sailors arriving in Bucksport, altering lives simply by their strangeness, envisions the charmed turmoil of the meeting of foreign voyager and local millworkers.

. . . The Bucksport girls
throw daisies to the Ecuadorians, who place them
behind their ears, and the officer sings about
a flower blooming in a forgotten place. The next
morning, the girls wear yellow flowers between
their breasts, but the sailors do not see them.
They want to shop in the American stores.

Like the sailors, the foreign tankers themselves are a reminder of years ago, when steamer and merchant sailing ship plied the bay and lines of towed schooners, five at a time, would be linked bow to stern like a train of elephants.

Several years ago, a Connecticut company looked at Bucksport and assumed that this mill town would complacently welcome their coal-fired energy plant. To their surprise, the town rebelled against the threat to their air and water, forcing the amazed company to retreat.

The snow is still on the ground as we finish our early coffee and head down through town on State 15 to the traffic light. Shortly beyond, in the cemetery across from the Shop 'n Save, the stain of a boot forever defiles Jacob Buck's tombstone, no matter how many times the grave marker is changed. He once sentenced a woman as a witch. Posterity seems to reveal just how powerful she was.

We now leave Bucksport, turning left at the light from the cemetery (right if you haven't stopped to visit), across the bridge to Verona Island, where Christmas decorations that include a sailboat have already been hung. We continue over the Waldo-Hancock Bridge, built in 1931. Were it summer, we would be watching for the osprey in the nest on the first tower we pass, now sparkling with snow. When the bridge was first built, volunteers were summoned to help remove snow after the bad storms. Once, they also needed volunteers to climb to the tops of the towers to chip the ice off the cables.

Tugs ease a tanker up the Penobscot River

Says James F. McAvoy, a former neighborhood resident now of Ophelia, Virginia, "As evidence of my weirdness at the time, I went up. I shall never forget that terrifying experience, nor would my mother ever let me forget it once she found out."

Across the river, Bucksport looks like the most charming of New England riverside towns, with its white clapboard homes and tall church steeples standing white within the white dusting. I forget how magical snow is in Maine. Perhaps Bucksport is the quintessential riverside town, solid and self-sufficient.

Before the bridge was built, people crossed the Penobscot River by the Prospect Ferry, north of Fort Knox. Because I live near here, sometimes at night I think of the ferry travelers of years ago, small and vulnerable beneath the great cliffs towering overhead. But then I also think the same of us in our camper truck, our home perched on our aging back, swaying on this great steel span above the river.

In Waldo County now, we turn right on State 174, heading west, away from the Penobscot River. The entrance to Fort Knox is on our right.

It is closed in winter, but those traveling in summer may not want to miss this large fort, built like a medieval castle overlooking the river, a maze of granite corridors, embankments, high stone arches, narrow windows squinting over the river, and deep, dank tunnels. One tunnel ends at the trail leading to the riverbank, an orgy of blackberries come August.

The fort was commissioned to protect Bangor in preparation for the Aroostook War, that never really was (see Chapter 9). That it is Maine's largest fortification, on 125 acres of land with walls sometimes forty feet thick, is a testament to the importance of the lumber industry at the time, and to the role of the Penobscot River as a crucial shipping artery for the port of Bangor. It was the last of its era in fort constructions. As architectural historians Frank Beard and Bette Smith write in *Maine's Historic Places*, "Nothing like it will ever be built again."

There may also be nothing in Maine like the gentle view over the river framed by the granite gunports of the fort. Watching a tanker come in one summer day, I remember my mind skipping over follies from past to future. Somehow, Fort Knox's grandiose absurdities seem to stand for the grand posturing of all wars, a multimillion-dollar echo of my little son's fierce karate stance as, what he calls, "Power Ranger X-Man Wolverine."

The road across to Prospect is a lovely woodland road, typical of the roads we will be traveling on this journey. This morning, it's still a wonderland of crystal. At Prospect we turn right again, onto US 1A north. The junction is marked by a red country store that rises up three stories. There used to be dances in the grange hall that tops the building. In fact, I believe Caro Hutchins (see Chapter 5) performed here. Downstairs, the store holds the basics: staples, candy, videos, and a pinball machine.

Just north of Prospect, as we approach the crest of the hill, I slow down to look to my right for the falls on the South Branch Marsh River. This rock-covered hill, the stream cascading to rapids below, with the high railroad bridge in the distance, is among my favorite spots in Maine. The deep, lush canyon, bathed in green in the summer and pure white now, hardly looks like Maine to me, or the United States, but like Europe—or like a European pastoral painting, perhaps by Gustave Courbet.

About two miles up the road, as the Marsh River widens near the Penobscot River, a small park and boat ramp are marked by granite blocks. These shores have been well quarried by treasure hunters: an old rumor, much disproven but still unquelled, places Captain Kidd's buried bounty here.

More recent treasure hunters have been seeking to discover the remains of the sunken ships of a great Revolutionary War naval disaster, when Commodore Dudley Saltonstall, Paul Revere, and other leaders with fine old New England names, commanding a total of forty ships, stalled so long in their attack that they let themselves be chased from Castine by four British vessels. Rather than surrender the bulk of the American navy, the captains set fire to their own ships. The affair led to court-martial proceedings and has been a hushed note of American naval history that's only now being faced, with the help of a hefty grant and waterborne archaeologists.

In Frankfort, the Marsh River is crossed by a little iron bridge, now laced in white, known as the Brooklyn Bridge. Across the bridge lies a small settlement on the slopes of a low hill covered with blueberries in August, a lovely spot for a gentle walk. Exploring on the far slopes, Bill and I once came upon an old house foundation with bits of pottery and weathered bottles. Frankfort may be a literal backwater—the water here backing into the Penobscot River—but like every town of its size, it has had its dramas. It was once mighty, before Prospect, Winterport, Hampden, and parts of Belfast, Searsport, and Stockton Springs broke away. And the Mount Waldo Granite Works here were once nationally known, supplying granite for buildings and paving blocks down the eastern seaboard and for the walls of Fort Knox.

There's a large, self-conscious portrait of the family of Albert L. Kelly of Frankfort by Jeremiah P. Hardy at the Farnsworth Museum in Rockland (see Chapter 4). Mrs. Kelly is wrapped in a red robe edged by ermine tails, fit for a queen; their very young son looks not to his parents, or the viewer, but up at a dizzying wall of law books.

We cross the Marsh River, only to return to it later on. Passing a gravel pit on our right, I stare to my left, driving slow. Nearly every morning one June, when I was traveling this road frequently, I saw a moose feeding at the far end of the marsh.

I doubt I'd see it now. Moose are most frequently seen along the roads in late April and early May, in the open ditches where the first greens of spring emerge. Beginning in June until moose hunting season in October, you can often see moose in a quiet pond or bog filled with greenery, where these majestic beasts munch away at the water plants, night and day. The moose are after salt, their sodium having been depleted over the long winter. Bog food is a sure antidote. Come winter, moose tend to head deep into the woods, in groups of six or so.

Upriver, we come to Winterport, whose name reflects its former prominence as the winter port for Bangor, when ice clogged the river farther up. Though sugar, hogsheads, butter, cheese, harnesses, and clothing were produced here and ships were built on the river, the town's importance was as a winter transfer station for the nineteenth-century boomtown of Bangor thirteen miles upriver. When the railroads came in, Winterport lost its importance, leaving the twentieth-century visitor the winner, for Winterport offers a strong presence of imposing homes and commercial buildings, now gathered into a historic district. The waterfront is still active, with a boatyard and cargo port.

From Winterport, we take State 139 west toward Monroe. The road begins as State 139/State 69, passing the Winterport Dragway, where men, women, and families come to race automobiles on summer weekends. State 139 soon branches left, a narrow ribbon meandering along the Marsh Stream, overhung by trees that have suddenly turned to crystal, shimmering in the sun.

At the top of a hill, just before we dip into Monroe, a right turn takes us to Stone Soup Farm. It may be hard to see the sign, but the farm is on the same road as the Red Barn. On a midsummer visit it offered a patchwork of perennial flowers and herbs scattered among soft hills. It closes in fall, but reopens near the holidays. Wreaths and gifts of herbs are packaged for sale, while tea is offered in the decorated tearoom.

Monroe is a close little community built between the north and south branches of the Marsh River, best introduced by the general store, with a display of dried beans beneath the counter, a little table offering one or two seats where visitors can drink their coffee, and a magazine rack displaying *Vegetarian Times*, *Organic Gardening*, *True Detective*, and *The Christian Woman*. Tucked in the ridges above town are a variety of establishments, including Common Courage, a left-wing publishing house with a national reputation; a cooperative land trust; and the homes of several artists and at least one midwife.

Also in Monroe is Monroe Salt Works, which produces salt-glazed pottery, located just north of the village. Outlets in Rockport, Searsport, and Ellsworth sell the pottery, but Ron Garfinkle welcomes visitors wishing to observe the entire process, from the making of the clay to the glazing of finished pots. The salt glaze is actually part of the firing process: when the kiln gets to peak temperature, around 2,200 degrees Farenheit, the door is opened and salt is thrown in, creating a vapor that produces the distinctive mottled glaze. To get to the pottery, turn right on the first paved road after the general store. At the sign "Pavement Ends," take a right; the pottery is about three-quarters of the way up the hill, on the left. Just the overlooks along these ridges are worth the detour.

State 139 is a good road for all seasons but heavy snow: luxurious in leaf, enchanting on a day like today when the light snow shimmers on the baubles of apples left on roadside trees. But heavy snow is not quickly removed here, and by late winter the tar rolls with frost heaves.

After Monroe, a bridge on the south side of the road is marked by blaze orange snowmobile signs. Off-season, this all-terrain-vehicle (ATV) trail is also a lovely walking path. We stretch our legs here briefly, our steps the first in the inch of snow mounded over each slat of the bridge. We emerge into a clearing where ice captures the arch of the trees, then return to our camper truck.

As we drive near the small Basin Pond, a coyote bolts across our path, reminding us of one amazing June ride here when we scared some wild turkeys gathering at the roadside, then stopped to help a small snapping turtle from one side of the road to the other. Then, at the Marsh Stream near Brooks, Bill saw a bittern land in the marsh and stopped the car. The bird hid itself, its sharp beak raised high, as if it were a reed.

We plan to turn north at Brooks, but we detour first on State 139 over the hill to Thorndike to look at pianos at Bryant Stove Works. We pass some old farmhouses, some ramshackle homes patched with tar paper, and some pitted trailers still in need of patching, reminiscent of 1930s America. In Thorndike, we pass the old train depot and cross State 220 where it junctions with State 139, driving into the Bryant Stove Works lot.

Bryant Stove Works, also known as the Bryant Stove Museum, is a large storehouse filled with cast-iron and enameled stoves for burning wood or coal, as well as a few pianos and many more mechanical pianos. Joe Bryant got into stoves after selling his steel fabrication business. How he got into pianos, especially player pianos, I'm not sure, but a few years back he decided they would be all the rage and launched into acquiring and restoring not only player pianos but nickelodeons and a circus calliope that plays music, bangs cymbals and drums, and also blows bubbles.

But player pianos didn't sell. His son Tim tells me that three years after Joe acquired the pianos, each of the eight Bryant children received one for Christmas. Since then, Joe, along with his wife, Beatrice (whom he goads with arguments over who is boss), have opened a museum in a large Quonset hut on the premises. On display are ten antique cars, eight nickelodeons, two band organs, and the one calliope.

While Bill and I discuss the pianos, Joe turns sorcerer, orchestrating the machines for our delighted little boy.

We leave reluctantly, noting that south of here, Schartner's Mount View Farms offers pick-your-own strawberries in June and July, followed by pick-your-own raspberries.

Heading back toward Brooks, I see a small cross on the rise of a hill, across from a farmhouse. There's a photo on the cross of a young boy; I don't know the story, but each time I pass that cross, no matter what I'm thinking, my mind shifts.

Back in Brooks, we turn north onto State 7 (a left turn for us, a right for those who haven't taken the detour to Thorndike). Farther north, this road is also known as the Moosehead Trail.

This is a straight-ahead road over hilly terrain. On this bright November day, from the top of one ridge we can see across to the next, seemingly miles ahead. We also see white painted farmhouses, black cows in barnyards, brown grass beginning to emerge from under the morning's snow, and views to the eastern hills beyond.

Soon we pass more crosses, these for Jackie Dodge Burnett, nineteen, and Kristy Gibbs, twelve. This time I know the story. They were cousins playing chicken in a car with some friends. They lost.

Ahead, there's a yellow barn attached not to an old farm-house but to a mobile home. Then we travel by more snow-covered fields surrounding a well-kept red house trimmed in white, a quintessential country image.

In Maine as elsewhere, the independent farmer has found it hard going. Even in rural Maine, life has become centralized. But farming was not necessarily isolating. There were community connections and also strong connections beyond Maine. Folks around Brooks, Unity, and Freedom used to milk their few cows in the morning, then send the milk to the rail station in Thorndike to be placed on the Boston-bound train.

A few years back, I spoke with a man named Harold "Red" Mitchell, born in 1910 and raised on a farm just ten miles south of here. "We had an apple orchard, we had a crop in the fall. Quite a lot of apples," said Red. "We picked them, packed them, put them in a cellar, and then the packers would come and they would grade them—number one or number two—and pack them into barrels and then we hauled them up with horses, took them up here to Thorndike, prob-ably, to the rails, or else off to the Boston boat, which used to come into Belfast. We didn't do it by trucks then. It was eleven miles to Thorndike, to the rails, or fourteen to fifteen miles to Belfast."

Maine farmers, who kept their farms quite diverse, often reserved the profits from apples to pay off taxes. In those days, cows were milked by hand, so ten cows would be the norm. Monthly payments were covered by the milk, hopefully.

Electricity came through in 1940. Before then, the milk was kept on ice that was cut from a river or pond. "You know, it was quite a job to put up the ice. You had to cut it and lug it with horses down the snow from some remote pond, some-where. Then you had to get sawdust to cover it on the sides, pack it, cover it all over for insulation. That's what kept it. And when you wanted a chunk of ice, you had to go in and shovel the sawdust off and break it up and take it in and wash it and clean it," said Red.

As we cross into Penobscot County just south of Dixmont, the northern view opens up even more. We pass a mailbox fashioned into a racing car, reminding us of the Winterport Dragway. Closer to Dixmont, with its inviting country store, the fields are dotted with large hay rolls, now damp from the melting snow, in preparation for delivery to various barns. Nearby, there's a colony of red shacks and a barn.

About five miles east of here, Piper Mountain Christmas Tree Farm has just opened its seasonal doors. We take a right down State 9/US 202 and watch on the right for Garland Road in about two miles. (If you miss it, take a right at Kennebec Road at the crossroads with State 143.) Before three miles have passed, we come to a large sign and a large white house. Between Thanksgiving and Christmas Eve, there is always a friendly greeter at the entrance, with a saw in hand. Inside the red barn, cider and doughnuts are served, and a range of trimmings are sold. Frequently, according to Heidi, who calls herself "just a daughter-in-law," carolers are about on weekend afternoons.

Back on State 7, Plymouth Pond suddenly appears on our right, set off by birch trees, golden with the autumn. State 7 traces the western shore of the pond, with swampland on our left. Then the road becomes a spectacular causeway over pond and marsh. On a rock, a bronze heron permanently watches for fish.

We have now come to the part of State 7 known as the Moosehead Trail. As we drive by a large connected farmhouse and barn, I see an old woman, weathered like her home, her back humped, hair straggling from a small net, her gait stooping as she walks out to post a letter. Did she, like Red Mitchell, once travel miles to school, walking in spring and fall, skiing in winter?

Just before Newport, we momentarily miss our road, continuing straight instead of turning left onto US 2/State 7/ State 100 to Newport. We turn around to get back on track.

If we had wanted only a limited backroad excursion, we could have taken I-95 to this point, exiting at Newport onto State 7 north.

I used to think of Newport as one of those towns that have suddenly mushroomed into an interchange, busy with ushering people off the highway and up to the north woods. But Newport, on the banks of the broad Sebasticook Lake, with its wide drainage basin, is an old Native American crossroads between Moosehead Lake, the Piscataquis River, and a number of locations along the Penobscot River. Indeed, Newport's name refers to the portage between the East Branch of the Sebasticook River and the tributaries of the Penobscot River; Sebasticook can be loosely translated as "the short route."

Today, I find nothing of the Native American or even French mission trails along the Sebasticook River, but a quick loop off the shopping and fast-food strip reveals a town of fine Victorian architecture. For the most part, the Victorian era was a profitable time for the lumbering industry, and many central and northern Maine towns revel in bits of Victorian gingerbread. Among the stars of Newport architecture is the Hexagon Barn on Spring and Railroad Streets, the only such agricultural oddity in the state, though there had been an octagonal barn in Dover-Foxcroft. It's attached to a Greek Revival farmhouse. To find it, we take a left at the light as we enter town, driving past Crosby's Funeral Home to Spring Street. Then we take a right. The barn is at the next corner, on Railroad and Spring Streets.

About a mile and a quarter after the traffic light marking the north end of Newport, we pass a sign for Noah's Ark, a zoo. It is closed now but was still open in September when we were driving this way. Inside, co-owner Patsy Tremblay explained how Newport happened to have a zoo.

"My son, Michael, always wanted a buffalo. From the time he was a little child, he always played cowboys and Indians and he would tell me, 'Some day, Mom, I'm going to have a buffalo.' "

But first he raced horses. Seeking to buy a horse one day, he saw a buffalo, bought her, then found her a mate.

What do you do with two buffalo? Open a zoo—what else? The senior Tremblays signed on, and together they accumulated an odd assortment of animals: a gibbon, with its own child-sized yellow and orange plastic picnic table; several antelope; a peacock; a raccoon; and a small playground for (human) children. But no more buffalo. After giving birth to three young ones, mother Diablo died of old age in November 1992. Her mate was later sold.

Despite the entrance through a store and the frequently small enclosures for the animals, I find myself charmed by the oddity of this tiny affair, gibbon and all, and await a return when the next buffalo appears.

We continue north, weathering minor engine trouble in the town of Corinna, dominated by the Eastland Woolen Mill.

The towns here are built around their mills and lakes. Guilford has its fabric mill, Hartland a tannery, Dexter its shoe factory, and Corinna has a food-processing plant in addition to Eastland, which produces wool for coats. There's a mill store in town where wool remnants are sold. Eastland is known for its loyal employees, most of whom were waiting to get their jobs back after a months-long layoff in 1993. Now, the mill is battling competition from the Ukraine.

Corinna is also known as the birthplace, in 1866, of Gilbert William Patten, who wrote the Frank Merriwell books under his pen name, Burt L. Standish. Perhaps no young boy will ever read them again, but Merriwell figured in my childhood, nay he still figures in my adulthood, for he was my father's hero. The Merriwell series was such a favorite boyhood companion that my father started a lending library in the basement of his Bronx apartment house solely to acquire more Merriwell adventures.

Patten was an awkward-looking child—over six feet tall and less than 115 pounds at age fourteen, an only child of religious folk who were more than forty when he was born. Stories were everything to him.

Corinna is also home to the Stewart Free Library, built by Levi M. Stewart, a native who became a millionaire in Minneapolis. This great Victorian structure, called "the pride of Corinna," was built in 1895 to honor Stewart's parents. In my wanderings, I've found that most towns have their own pride of a library, often the most interesting structure in town.

Dexter, too, has a substantial library, and its mills. According to *Maine: A Guide Downeast*, Dexter thrived in the latter part of the nineteenth century. Whereas other Maine towns lost population after the Civil War, French-Canadian immigrants swelled Dexter's rolls. A railroad came here, up from Newport—the Dexter and Newport Railroad.

Until recently, when the mill was sold, Dexter was also the home of the oldest family-owned mill in the United States, the Amos Abbott Company Mill, founded in 1820 and managed by the same family for five generations. It produced "Abbott grays," which were said to "wear like iron." One Abbott son had a full career directing art museums before returning home to manage the mill. Jere Abbott was associate director of the then-fledgling Museum of Modern Art in New York City, then ran the art museum at Smith College before taking over the mill in the 1940s. Back in Maine, he connected with the Colby College Museum of Art, in Waterville, to which he left $2 million as an endowment for acquisitions—a hefty sum for a college museum.

But our interests now are more concrete. We need to eat. We stop at a park on Lake Wassookeag, just outside of Dexter, and practically inhale our sandwiches. Our timing is wrong, because I've heard that Dexter's public suppers are worth staying around for, especially the chicken pies.

We continue north and slightly east on State 7 toward Dover-Foxcroft, passing a flag the size of a house, then several tiny houses and some old trailers.

About fourteen miles north of Dexter, we take a left near a brick house onto Burough Road, just south of Dover-Foxcroft, and drive for 1.5 miles seeking an enchanted forest. Here, what began as a Halloween figure thirty-five years ago has burgeoned into a four-acre grove filled with chainsaw sculptures. "Charles" was a Halloween ornament that Ardell Flanders, a retired dairy farmer, carved from pine with a chainsaw. Later, Charles became a scarecrow. Then a unicorn appeared by a path in the pine grove. His wife liked it and the figures kept coming. Flanders welcomes visitors, thousands every summer, including busloads of children who swarm over the playground rides he has created from farm machinery. There's a Noah's ark here, too; the animals move in when the crank is turned on their boat, the bed of a silage chopper. But now we just look from the truck; Ardell closes the forest come hunting season and reopens after mud season in the spring.

We follow this road until it meets the Sangerville Road, where we take a left and pass several family-owned farms raising vegetables and Christmas trees in the Piscataquis River valley. Midway along this river, Low's Covered Bridge, a 125-foot bridge built in 1830 and washed out in a 1987 flood, has already been rebuilt and restored.

At Sangerville, the road plunges downhill to the town that was the birthplace of Sir Hiram Maxim, knighted by Queen Victoria in 1901 for his prolific inventions, among them the machine gun. He is also said to have missed obtaining the lightbulb patent by a day. His younger brother, Hudson, patented smokeless gunpowder in the United States, engendering a feud between the two gifted inventors who grew up in deep poverty outside of Sangerville. Late in life, Hudson dictated memories of his boyhood for "Hudson Maxim: Reminiscences and Comments," excerpted in Charles and Samuella Shains's wonderful book *Growing Up in Maine*. These passages disclose some of the rigors buried within these old farmhouse walls:

> The roof leaked more or less, but wasn't as bad as the sides of the house, in which were great cracks right through to the outer elements. These let the winter storms beat in, and we'd wake up in the morning and find our heads covered with snow.
> Lack of shoes didn't prevent my going to school, except in the very severest weather; and my two younger brothers went with me, no better shod. We could go on the hard snow and ice much better than we could through a light snow, because the light snow would get up inside our trousers on our bare legs, which couldn't stand it so well as our feet. The way we managed was to run with all our might as long as our feet could endure the cold, and then climb up on a fence, or sit down on a boulder or a stump, and rub

our feet and ankles with our hands; and then we'd rush on again.

We take a right through town and over the arched green metal bridge for the mill town of Guilford, home of Guilford Industries. At the edge of Maine's northern woods, Guilford produces wool panels for urban offices and polyester blankets. With its large brick library, large woolen mill, and quiet riverside walk, Guilford exudes prosperity born from industry. A mill store in town sells the ends of the panels and other fabrics.

Nearby stands a wonderfully ornate Queen Anne house built around 1885 by David Robinson Straw, Jr., lawyer and insurance executive. According to Beard and Smith's *Maine's Historic Places*, the house rivals any such building in Maine. Now painted deep brown with yellow trim, it has become the Trebor Inn Bed and Breakfast.

Guilford Industries was owned by Willard and Helen Cummings. Like the Abbotts of Dexter, the Cummingses were art collectors. Their son, portrait artist Willard Cummings, cofounded the Skowhegan School of Painting and Sculpture on Lake Wesserunsett, southwest of Guilford, a summer retreat-like school where noted artists come to critique, lecture, and work alongside emerging artists.

To the west, just after the bridge takes traffic back over the river, the town has created a quiet, lovely, riverside walk. Beyond, the road is now a combination of State 6, 15, and 16. We stop for tea at the Wagon Wheel Restaurant, which bills itself as "the good food place with the big plates." In the booth behind us sits a substantial man eating a substantial steak. Bill strikes up a conversation with him, and we discover a roads enthusiast unlike any I had ever met: his hobby is driving and his ambition is to drive every road in the state, his favorites being the northern toll roads used by logging trucks.

In the large back room of the Wagon Wheel—tables are arranged as if for a convention. We are told that late last night, which was a Saturday night, after the hunters had their dinner, the tables were cleared away and local women joined the men in a wild dance party. For a moment, I lament traveling on Sunday, a decision made specifically to avoid worries over hunters.

At Abbot Village the road forks and we leave State 16 for State 6/State 15 north. I am looking forward to Titcomb's Store, a great old country store with rooms opening farther and farther back into different realms—from toys to kitchen gadgets to sporting goods. But we arrive in Abbot to find the store closed. The last time we were in the area, the store had been bought by a young couple from Ohio. Apparently, it was too much for the young couple—or too little by way of reward. I didn't think I had been in Maine long enough to watch parts of it shut down, but here I am. Now, the nearest such store I know of is on Indian Hill, just before Greenville.

Nearby is Elderberry Inn, another of Maine's farm bed and breakfasts, with a handful of farm animal pets, including two potbelly pigs, Agatha and Goober. The farm is on 185 acres near the Piscataquis River. There are hiking trails here, but after this morning's snow, I look forward to the cross-country ski trails, and even the wild thrill of snowmobiling through territory we could never begin to see with Daniel's limited stamina on skis.

Continuing north to Monson, one of the first images is the Kennedy Slate Company on our right, housed in an old white-tiled gas station filled to the brim with piles of slate. There is something incongruous about this gas station filled with stone, as if the earth had decided to take back its resource, the rock rising up to claim its fuel.

Slate is the bedrock of Monson and the broader region north of here. Slate quarries are scattered throughout the area. Southeast on North Guilford Road (the one that enters Monson at the Kennedy Slate Company's gas station) is Sheldon Slate Products, Inc., the largest enterprise here. Formerly known as the Portland and Monson Slate Company, or the Monson Slate Company, this outfit supplied the slate to mark all the Kennedy graves, including the half-ton slab of black slate for the grave of Jacqueline Kennedy Onassis in Arlington National Cemetery.

Begun in 1906, Sheldon Slate Products operated the first mines in the area, employing many Swedes. Not infrequently, workers in these dusty mines died young of silicosis.

Around 1927, the slate was transported on a narrow-gauge railroad five miles from Monson to Monson Junction. Today, those tracks stand in the Boothbay Railway Village (Chapter 5).

On the shores of Lake Hebron at the edge of Monson, the great photographer Berenice Abbott lived for many years until her death in December 1991. She lived to be ninety-three. Unable to photograph for much of her last years, she feistily motored her Boston Whaler along the shores of Lake Hebron, her short-cropped gray hair circumscribing a face of ageless determination. "I think there's nothing smarter than an old woman," she said, just months before her death, to some producers who were filming a video of her life.

The hills around here are also the realm of artist Alan Bray, a native of Monson, now living near Sangerville, who has received wide attention for his work. He paints these trees and hills with such painstaking realism that he finds the ghosts of the past within them, creating haunting, almost eerie scenes that may begin with the local landscape but end with the projection of an inner, surrealistic dream.

The road now leads directly north to Greenville, the famous frontier town at the edge of Moosehead Lake and the north woods. But on this suddenly gray day, we have chosen another destination. Northeast of Monson lies Boarstone Mountain. These hills are not well known, so there is something intensely alluring in the intimacy here. We feel like explorers.

To get there, we look for signs for the Boarstone Mountain Preserve, a right turn one-quarter of a mile north of the center of Monson on what becomes Elliotsville Road. Be warned: it eventually becomes a dirt road, indeed a rough road at times. It is also superbly beautiful here, as we head into dark mountains, along roads lined with birches, their white bark glowing in beams breaking through the clouds, with no leaves to shield them. Their golden leaves are strewn over the dirt path, which is dotted in crevices by unmelted snow. As we edge closer to Boarstone, we drive along the Big Wilson Stream on our right before crossing it at a cascading waterfall.

At the waterfall, we have the choice of turning left for Bodfish Road to hike Boarstone Mountain or bearing right toward Lake Onawa. We choose the lake first, proceeding down the road and then taking a turnoff to the left onto Onawa Road. We pass several mailboxes, and a sign for the F. J. F. Building Company here, leading to the Lake Onawa boat ramp. A view out to Greenwood Pond and then the railroad tracks confirm that we're on the right path.

This is a remarkable place. When we get to the boat ramp (unmarked but paved) on this bleak, misting day, now fully clouded, I think of a Tibetan sanctuary. The surrounding mountains—Barren and Benson and the steep, conical peak of Boarstone, raised like a nightcap into the sleepy sky—are themselves surrounded by long wisps of clouds. Every cloud, mountain, and shred of fog, every island, tree, and moss-covered rock finds its mirrored partner in the perfectly still lake.

But Lake Onawa is not undiscovered. Some twenty-five camps front its waters, many approachable only by boat. Down the road from the boat ramp (and a short walk from an

Floatplanes are sometimes the easiest way to commute among Maine lakes

automobile turnaround) there's the little settlement of Onawa. It was built alongside the railroad tracks of the Canadian Pacific line, about a mile in each direction from the ramp that leads to the lake and the imposing, seventy-seven-foot-high railroad trestle that spans a narrow edge of it accessible by a footpath continuing beyond this enclave.

Once upon a time, Onawa, like several other settlements in northern Maine, arose pridefully alongside the Canadian Pacific tracks, depending upon a tiny schoolhouse for education, a large community hall for entertainment, and the rails for its roads. There were no other roads. And none other were necessary. Even rail strikes couldn't isolate the communities, for a handcar would still operate. Nowadays, this is mostly a summer community, but chimney smoke, electric lights, and laundry hung out and dampening in the November mist attest to current habitation.

This is no ghost town; rather it looks like a model-railway hamlet, with houses built into hills that stand hard by the rails, purple kale still bright at a railside garden, and at least one home under construction. This one is sided with cedar shingles that are cut and placed so as to create a mosaic facade with a great shining sun surrounded by leaves. This home looks as lovingly crafted as any set onto a miniature railway layout. Artist Kathy Ready fashioned the design on the house, her home, before she died of medical complications a few years ago. The building was once the general store.

I've been told that Lake Onawa is almost incomparable for fishing; a fishing party I know of caught "one of each kind" in the lake. Even their four-year-old was reeling them in.

Our near-four-year old (lacking a fishing rod) reveled in the idea of a canoe trip to one of the tiny islands that dot the lake. But noticing the towering cone of Boarstone Mountain, he turned intrepid explorer. "I want to climb that mountain" became his refrain.

To get to Boarstone we return the four to five miles from the boat ramp at Lake Onawa to the "main" road and turn right at the Wilson Stream Bridge. Borestone's trailhead is about two miles north on that road. The trail itself is a steep one, taking us up the rest of the 2,000-foot mountain in about 2.5 miles of walking.

Mountain aficionados may notice that the Appalachain Mountain Club lists this as Boarstone Mountain, but that spelling is incorrect, according to Jack Dunstan, the managing warden of the mountain. He tells two legends about the name. Boarstone was originally called Bore Mountain and changed to Borestone because it reminded people of Scotland and the borestone that standards were once set upon. "Being a Scot, I like that," says Jack. The other concerns R. T. Moore, the owner of the mountain, and his friend, a sponsor of the Appalachian Trail through Maine. "He asked Moore whether the trail could go over Borestone Mountain and Moore agreed." But this friend was also a friend of someone down at the U.S. Geological Survey in Washington and had the name changed to Boarstone. "When Moore found out, he ordered the man and his trail off the mountain," adds Jack. The Appalachian Trail now travels around Boarstone and over Barren Mountain. But Dunstan demurs: "Now these are legends, and I can't swear that they are true, but Moore was an articulate man and not a person to play around with," he says.

Near the top of the mountain is another reminder of the wiles of history: the ruins of the Boarstone Mountain Fox Company, Inc.

Near the spot where Sunset, Midday, and Sunrise Ponds skip across the boulders, R. T. Moore raised about a hundred fox a year, selling the furs down in the cities. His wife, a concert pianist, brought her Steinway grand piano up the mountain one winter and across a frozen pond to the encampment's main lodge. In summer, the Moores entertained guests with piano concerts and tennis tournaments on their mountainside courts.

In addition to being one of the most successful fox farmers in the nation, Moore was also an amateur ornithologist. When he died in 1958, he left Boarstone Mountain, all of which he owned and none of which he cut, to the National Audubon Society.

Relics of the fox farm remain, but Jack Dunstan warns that the farm is off limits. Partially, it's the danger: boulders hide deep holes into the rocky mountain that could swallow a child whole, and leftover wire could gash a leg. But Dunstan is also protecting vegetation, such as rare and delicate lichen that take twenty-five years to grow an inch. Dunstan asks that guests stop at the visitors center, once the Moores' garage, and stay on the trails. He also suggests that cold-weather visitors notify him before they leave for Boarstone and again when they come off the mountain. He's worried about the quick temperature drops—as much as fourteen degrees in ten minutes.

It is a rugged climb, but spectacular, as mountain after mountain opens up in this rather uncharted region to the east, where the railroad is the only path.

Back down the mountain, we could either return to Monson and continue north to Greenville, or take an adventurous trip east from Dover-Foxcroft to Milo to West Enfield to link with the Aroostook trip (see Chapter 9), or simply return south through Willimantic to State 150 and Guilford, where State 23 leads to Dexter and then State 7 to Newport.

In the Area

Champion paper mill, Bucksport, 207-469-1700.
Northeast Historic Film, Bucksport, 207-469-0924.

Crosby's Drive-In, Bucksport, 207-469-3640.

The Dockside Restaurant, Bucksport, 207-469-7389.

MacLeod's Restaurant, Bucksport, 207-469-3963.

Jed Prouty Motor Inn, Bucksport, 207-469-3113.

Fort Knox, Prospect, 207-469-7719.

Sail Inn Restaurant, Prospect, 207-469-3850.

Waldo Pierce Library, Frankfort, 207-223-5324.

Winterport Dragway, Winterport.

Colonial Winterport Inn, Winterport, 207-223-5307.

Monroe General Store, Monroe, 207-525-3540.

Monroe Salt Works, Monroe, 207-525-4471.

Stone Soup Farm, Monroe, 207-525-4463.

Bryant Stove Shop and Museum, Thorndike, 207-568-3665.

Schartner's Mount View Farms, Thorndike, 207-568-3668.

Oz's General Store, Dixmont, 207-234-3943.

Piper Mountain Christmas Tree Farm, Dixmont,
207-234-4300.

Noah's Ark, Newport, 207-368-2136.

Lake Sebasticook Bed and Breakfast, Newport,
207-368-5507.

Eastland Woolen Mill Factory Outlet, Corinna, 207-278-8900.

Stewart Free Library, Corinna, 207-278-2454.

Abbott Memorial Library, Dexter, 207-924-7292.

Dexter Shoe Company, Dexter, 207-924-7341.

Ardell Flanders, woodcarver, Dover-Foxcroft, 207-564-7514.

Guilford of Maine, Guilford, 207-876-3331, store
207-876-3829.

Trebor Inn Bed and Breakfast, Guilford, 207-876-4070.

Elderberry Inn, Abbot, 207-876-4901.

Wagon Wheel Restaurant and Lounge, Inc., Abbot,
207-876-3712.

Monson Historical Museum, Monson, 207-997-3792.

Kennedy Slate Company, Monson, 207-997-9617

Sheldon Slate Products Company, Inc., Monson,
207-997-3617.

Jack Dunstan, Boarstone Mountain warden, 207-997-3558.

7 ~

One of the World's Beauty Spots

Getting there: From southern Maine, take I-95 to Augusta, then take State 3 to Belfast and US 1/State 3 north to Bucksport.

Highlights: *Historic Castine and Blue Hill; hiking in the Holbrook Island Sanctuary; four reversing falls; the working fishing town of Stonington and kayaking among the offshore islands; Haystack Mountain School of Crafts; and the WoodenBoat School.*

The roads through Blue Hill and Deer Isle wind around blueberry barrens that fall stains a deep red and that spring fires, set to promote greater production, char black.

There is a harsh beauty here. Rocks and boulders are scattered over the prickly hills, as if long ago some giant had been playing marbles on the land and had neglected to pick up the rough, primitive balls. But then, after passing through such primordial landscape, the road will shift toward a lake or bay and the world will open to a wrenchingly beautiful quartet of tree, rock, sea, and sky.

"Even the wildflowers seem to have a more piercingly beautiful color," writer Helen Yglesias once told me, trying to explain the lure of Blue Hill. She has joined the many artists, writers, and musicians living in the area she has called "one of the beauty spots of the world."

For its mixture of population and occupations, for its beauty and reserve, for its towns of white clapboard homes and its fields of cricket-laden hay spreading to the shore, this is quintessential coastal Maine. Yet it's enough off the main path that its most well-known native may have been a pig. No, not Rosebud, but Wilbur, the one given to posterity by E. B. White in *Charlotte's Web*. White was a summer resident, but like many seasonal refugees he eventually chose to live in the area full-time.

There is not much distance covered on this journey, but there is much to see and do. These roads can be driven in one day, but whenever I come here I find I want to settle down for life. Three days might be a reasonable compromise.

One warning: the roads here tangle. State 175 and State 176, especially, play hide-and-seek with each other. Direction north or south on any one portion of a road is relative. This is circular territory.

We take a circular route, covering much of the region moving south and north as we travel more or less west to east, from Castine to Cape Rosier to Blue Hill to Deer Isle and Stonington. As on the previous trip, we begin this journey in Bucksport. There are two choices for highway access from southern Maine: either I-95 to Augusta, picking up State 3 east to Belfast and US 1/State 3 north to Bucksport, or I-95 to Bangor, exiting on I-395 to State 15 south to Bucksport.

It is a hot day in June cooled by a gentle breeze as Bill, Daniel, and I leave US 1/State 3 in Bucksport turning right down State 175 toward Castine.

We begin in Orland, a town that always feels immensely complete, with its river, church, and stalwart old houses. The roadside sparkles a starry blue from forget-me-nots. State 175 here hugs close to the shore of the Penobscot River. As we look to the right, it's not the mainland we see, but Verona Island, lodging like an arrowhead into the mouth of the Penobscot River.

We continue straight toward Castine on State 166 when State 175 turns left toward Blue Hill. Then, at the Y where State 166 and 166A split, we bear right onto State 166A for Castine.

The road shifts inland here, over marshy land studded with historic homes, then rejoins State 166 toward the village. Then, between two Federal homes standing sentinel on the hillside, the road dips and water encroaches from both sides. Here is the neck of the Castine peninsula. The water to our left, looking like a lake now but like a mudflat at low tide, is Hatch Cove, part of the Bagaduce River, which divides Castine from the rest of the Blue Hill peninsula.

We lost Castine and much of downeast Maine during the War of 1812. The British captured it, securing it by building a canal across this neck, turning Castine into an island.

That fight for Castine was but the last of 200 years of fighting over this elegant town with its excellent harbor. After Europeans wrested the region from Native Americans, the French, Dutch, British, and Americans all wanted it—and each had it, at least for a time.

Now only a partial canal, the area where men once battled over nationhood by water is traversed by a road. To our left, the fields leading to Hatch Cove are covered with lupine. To our right, at Wadsworth Cove along the Penobscot River, children dig in the rough, pebbly sand and splash in the sun-warmed water.

There's a lot of complicated history here, and many great stories. Jean-Vincent d'Abbadie de Saint-Castin, a Frenchman, is featured in many early Castine legends. Castin, a second son of noble birth, came to the new world as a soldier because his elder brother was in line for the inheritance. Assigned to the fort at Pentagoet (the pre-Castin name for Castine), he married Mathilde, the daughter of Native American chief Madockawando. Then Castin amassed a fortune through trading. In those days, it was the British and the French who were fighting over the territory. The scheming was great. Eventually, the French lost Castine, but the town retained its French name.

Later, during the War of Independence, in the story referred to in Chapter 6, several of the colonial navy's best leaders lost their nerve and so their reputations, first gathering a fleet to take Castine, then believing that the British, holed up with barely a gun among them, were acting from strength. American hesitation lasted so long that the British reinforcements arrived to chase the Americans up the Penobscot, forcing them to burn their vessels.

After the British lost Castine in the War of Independence, Castine lost much of its population and even some of its buildings. Loyalists, unable to remain in the country they fought, slid their homes onto barges and sailed north, to Saint Andrews, New Brunswick, which remained comfortably loyal to the crown. I've been to Saint Andrews. There, among streets of staid old capes, is the rest of Castine, each home with a historic marker giving the date the structure was towed to its new site.

Castine is yet another town preserved by its loss of transportation. No longer essential as a commercial harbor, Castine has experienced minimal twentieth-century impact. But it is still a favorite harbor for pleasure boats. At the height of the season, yachts tie up two abreast at Eaton's Boat Yard, and cashmere cardigans dangle from leather bags as Castine's visitors take their evening strolls. But unlike Camden or Bar Harbor, Castine is too far down a side road to feel crowded, or beset by tourist shops.

The Castine town green

Visitors come here, as the proprietor of Compass Rose, the local bookstore, explains—not tourists. And, I might add, poets and artists. Here was the summer home of Robert Lowell during the years he was married to Elizabeth Hardwick. She still keeps a house on a bluff overlooking the Bagaduce River. Mary McCarthy lived here, too, for many years. Poet Philip Booth occupies an ancestral home among the Federal buildings that line Main Street's descent to the harbor. Centuries ago, painter Fitz Hugh Lane worked in the moss green home on Main Street, the one with the mansard roof. Now, sculptor Clark Fitz-Gerald lives at the tip of Castine, just beyond the lighthouse at Dice Head.

Any preciousness that might affect Castine is seasoned by a hint of scruffiness at the waterfront, helped along by the presence of the Maine Maritime Academy, which trains students for marine-related careers. Their hangout (and one of my son's very favorite places) is the Reef, a bar and pool hall facing the docks. For lunches, we also like Bah's Bakehouse, with indoor as well as outdoor dining, on its raised deck in the green building behind Main Street.

Both architecture and history call for a walking tour. Signs line the roads noting historic buildings; an annotated map is available beside almost every cash register in town. Main Street is a logical beginning. It is lined with multiple-chimneyed nineteenth-century Federal and Greek Revival homes, many with lovely side gardens. The three-story, three-season Castine Inn, lovingly renovated by Mark Hodesh, Margaret Parker, and Kathy Gould, offers dining with a seasonal theme. The story of the inn, and its kitchen secrets, are captured in *Recipes from a Down East Inn* by Country Roads Press.

At the end of town, the Dice Head Lighthouse is no longer lit, but a public path nearby leads through a meadow to the rocky shore, where an operating, industrial-strength light is perched on the hard nose of Castine. Searsport and Belfast shimmer across the bay.

Standing here, looking beyond the swoop of Islesboro to the Camden Hills and a mirage of islands on the southern horizon, my perspective of Maine alters and I can begin to understand Castine as it was 175 and 200 years ago, at the hub of a coastal arc of power, and very hotly contested.

Leaving town, we take State 166, passing in succession some historic homes, an old barn fully tumbled down, and many farmhouses with large fields spread out over the hills. We turn right onto State 199. Near the Bagaduce Narrows, we pass a house kneeling almost in the road, and on our left, we see a pond harboring a fleet of miniature lobster boats. Soon after, there's a mailbox created in the form of a deer.

We've come now to the apex of the Bagaduce River's Northern Bay, where State 175 and 199 overlap. At the tiny town of Penobscot, State 199 turns north to US 1. But we stay on State 175, heading to South Penobscot.

In town—a tiny, charming enclave—an artist couple share a building displaying David Larson's paintings on the second story. Below, a partnership of three weavers offers textiles and gifts at North Country Textiles. The store also has a branch in Blue Hill.

I'm told there's good Maine crabmeat in the local market.

Barely two miles out of town, we come upon one last British landmark—a bright-red London double-decker bus parked in the woods and serving fish and chips, seasonally, during afternoon hours, called The Real Thing!

From here we embark on a long drive through Brooksville and Cape Rosier. Were we interested in a less thorough tour of the Blue Hill region, we would take State 177 directly to the town of Blue Hill. But we continue on State 175, then turn right where State 175/State 176 veers onto the Brooksville peninsula. (Remember, these are circular roads.)

As we cross the bridge over the Bagaduce River, I look down at the water. If we're near the cusp of the tide, either way, the river churns beneath us, a reversing falls formed by the funneling of the river through the narrows here and into the Upper Bagaduce, creating something of a backwash. Canoeists and kayakers ride the rapids under the bridge, letting the tide wash them back to try it again, a perpetual motion of rapids until the tide slackens. This seems to be a feature of the region; we will pass three more reversing falls on this trip.

At the reversing falls is the Bagaduce Lunch, open in summer only, where customers take their orders of fried clams or lobster rolls to eat at picnic tables overlooking the falls. Friends of ours make this a summer feast, bringing chilled champagne, salad, and sliced fresh strawberries to accompany the fried clams.

Here is the northernmost Atlantic breeding ground for the horseshoe crab. We can often find these strange, primordial, olive-green creatures or their egg cases along the shore.

At the T, the road splits to circle the Brooksville section of the peninsula. We take a right, onto State 176 toward West Brooksville, following around until we come to a sign directing us toward the Holbrook Island Sanctuary and Cape Rosier.

The road here rises above Smith Cove, then cuts across the cape to Holbrook. A sign on the road promises a picnic area, which we visit, driving down a steep hill to the cove. Coming back to water again after this long, circuitous ride, we look out to see that we are quite close to where we started. Castine is just a skip of a skiff across the way. The water has so carved this land that cars seem to be an impediment to quick movement. Indeed, people who live here frequently do use their boats as vehicles, at least for commutes to Castine. We climb the hill again, continuing our journey to Holbrook, which is down the road on our right.

At Holbrook, a right turn leads to part of the sanctuary. Across a narrow bay, Holbrook Island completes the public park.

This nature sanctuary is wild, coastal territory, a mixture of forest, marsh, field, and barrens. I've hiked and skied here, finding a path to an icy stretch of water, when summertime's close palette of blue and black and green is pared away, and vistas are down to green, black, and winter's scouring white.

And yet, my thoughts at Holbrook seldom focus entirely on nature. It is Anita Harris who dominates my mind.

Harris was the crotchety, wealthy, and ultimately heroic donor of Holbrook. For years, she lived by herself on Holbrook Island. When neighbors on the mainland died, she developed a habit of buying their land—and razing their vacant homes. She never wanted to see the hand of man or woman. Democratic to the end, she stipulated the same be done with her own home when she passed on.

Like a family secret that everyone knows and no one discusses, these destroyed homes loom large in the sanctuary. We come upon yet another one now, the remains of a huge shingle-style cottage plowed into its own foundation, chunks of mortared brick and walls of shingles strewn across a field where once a garden bloomed. For half an hour, we reconstruct the layout—toilet and kitchen, fireplace and cellar—now fragments of an aristocratic past.

Something of Anita Harris's wealth, arrogance, and single-minded focus is captured in Robert Lowell's monumental poem "Skunk Hour," though Lowell used poetic license to turn her from a resident of Holbrook Island into "Nautilus Island's hermit heiress . . ."

> Thirsting for
> the hierarchic privacy
> of Queen Victoria's century,
> she buys up all
> the eyesores facing her shore,
> and lets them fall.

Leaving Holbrook, we take a right toward Goose Falls, the second reversing falls and another lookout onto Castine. Here, there's a little bridge and something of a waterworks. Nearby, a slag heap points to the remains of a copper mine. Harris adamantly opposed it, and with good reason. It was not profitable and was quickly abandoned, but not before creating this massive gray heap.

Beyond here is Harborside, which Helen and Scott Nearing turned into a pilgrimage site for back-to-the-landers. They wrote about "living the good life," taking control of one's life, living simply, wholly, and with discipline, parceling time for active work and time for contemplation. Helen carries on the good life she and Scott forged, in the house they built of stone that they cleared from the land. The house is visible on the left as we drive south on Goose Falls Road.

My connection to the Nearings is older, though. Scott Nearing always said, "Do the best you can in the place where you are and be kind." Before coming to Maine, he taught in New York City, where he created what he called a Free School for workers in the sweatshops. There, after a full day of stitching in the factory, the mostly immigrant workers would soak up his thinking. Among them was my feisty, clearheaded Great Aunt Miriam, now over ninety-four years old.

This road leads to the Head of the Cape, but the views are privately owned. From the water, Cape Rosier is a high, hard nub of land, heavily forested but dotted with modern mansions. From the land, these new homes, most likely products of 1980s investment booms, are known only by pale dirt roads scarring the woods. It is possible to follow the edge of the cape, but there's not much to see except new-growth forest. I prefer to turn the car around after Harborside and take the older Cape Rosier Road, which bisects the central two miles of the cape. We look for the road coming in on our right and take it, then make a left across the top of Weir Cove.

Our next right, at a sign advertising Metinic Yacht Corporation, leads to Horseshoe Cove, a small, almost mysterious cut in the cape snaking almost as far as Smith Cove. This is a good place to visit with a small motorboat, canoe, kayak, or rowboat, but the tide can be a menace. The lower falls drop four feet at low tide. At high tide, almost 1.5 miles of cove lie beyond the boatyard, and the falls will hardly be felt. But we took our dinghy with a light outboard here one summer evening in an attempt to shoot the falls (1.5 hours before and one hour after high tide are best), and then almost couldn't get back because the tide was so strong.

At the next major intersection, Cape Rosier Road meets Goose Falls Road. These roads are not well marked, so we must pay attention to our bearings or we can be sent back around the cape. A right turn gets us off the cape; a right again gets us on State 176 toward South Brooksville. The long blue-green bay we pass after turning onto State 176 is Orcutt Harbor, foretelling the entrance to South Brooksville.

Here, at Buck's Harbor, is the town immortalized by Robert McCloskey in *One Morning in Maine*. Farther out in the bay is the region of *Time of Wonder*. Perhaps little Sal and her father rowed over from the Scott Islands, out past Little Deer Isle, where McCloskey himself lives. Perhaps they came from closer in. South Brooksville looks much the same as it did in McCloskey's 1952 illustrations, with the grocery store and Condon's Garage little changed. Nearby, a squadron of ducks squawks at all intruders. At the waterfront (and not part of McCloskey's book), a large, shingle-style yacht club caters to summer sailors. Thursday night is folk-dance night. The first set is for the preschoolers and the second for the school-aged children; by the third hour young teenagers take hold, haughtily avoiding each other's glances as they show off their steps.

Peering around town, I see signs for the Bagaduce Chorale's twentieth anniversary. The chorale is one of several noted amateur musical ensembles on the Blue Hill peninsula (the Surrey Opera Company and two amateur steel-drum bands—Flash in the Pan and Bagaduce Steel Band being the others).

Mary Cheyney Gould, a former keyboard soloist with the Toledo (Ohio) Symphony Orchestra, is the woman behind the chorale. She came to Brooksville to retire and found that in this rather remote area, population 800, three homes had twin grand pianos. Soon Gould was playing duets and organizing the chorale.

In 1983, Gould, along with associates Fritz Jahoda and Marcia Chapman (who herself later organized the Bagaduce Steel Band), created the Bagaduce Music Lending Library, a unique national library that lends musical scores and also helps to find obscure ones. For years, the library lived in Gould's Brooksville garage. Now, it's housed in larger quarters on State 172 in Blue Hill.

We continue south, hugging the coast as a sailor might. We take State 176 to Brooksville, then turn right onto State 175, then right again onto State 175/State 15 beyond Walker Pond, toward Sargentville.

The road soon climbs Caterpillar Hill, a vast ridge rolling over scrubby blueberry barrens that tumble to a shimmering Walker Pond. Beyond lies Eggemoggin Reach and its scattering of islands. Edging the far distance, the Camden Hills lend a flat gray-green presence to the horizon mist.

We stop for an ice cream at the Country View Restaurant, relishing the heat of this late June day.

After Caterpillar Hill, the road comes to a T, with State 175 heading left and back around to Sedgwick and State 15 pushing on to Deer Isle. We take that right turn onto State 15 for Deer Isle.

Be prepared for yet another stunning vista—the breathtaking arch of the Deer Isle bridge, seemingly reaching to heaven. This is a bridge so long and high that it sometimes quivers in the wind. In very strong winds, it is closed.

The bridge was built in 1939, forging links between Deer Isle and the mainland. Still, Deer Isle can't help but be isolated: it's nearly an hour from movie theaters, malls, and the trappings of modernity. The region may even have had more external connections before the bridge came in—when Stonington was bustling with merchant ships and granite quarries and travel by sea was common. But though only 25,000 Mainers still work the waters, the seas still are an essential part of life here; look at the brilliant colors of the many lobster buoys bobbing along the coast.

We turn right off the bridge for a short trip to the public boat landing at the end of Eggemoggin Road. From here, we can look back at where we've been—across the reach to Buck's Harbor in South Brooksville, and beyond to Cape Rosier. For us, there's the thrill and tug of the water: these are the seas we sail. Exploring by land becomes a means of filling the gaps, seeing close up what we peer at through binoculars.

The Eggemoggin Inn is a lovely old place with gracious porches. Though more disheveled from land than it appears from the water, it offers a taste of that blessed life of the summer visitor, yet another population group on the island.

Returning from Eggemoggin, we take State 15 over one of Maine's most magnificent paths, a causeway bordered by beach, sea, and miniature islands between Little Deer Isle and Deer Isle. We savor this spot, stopping for a moment at the end of the causeway to breathe this beauty of rock and sea.

State 15 continues through to Stonington, but there are always detours. A sign for the Inn at Ferry Landing lures us more for the idea of seeing the old ferry landing than for seeing the inn. So we take a left on the road marked Ferry Road to a spot where gravel leads to water, the remains of the old ferry landing. We also stop to speak to the inn's owner, John Deis, who recently moved here from eastern Long Island.

The inn is an old one, used by travelers during the days of the ferry. This one also had a general store; a lounge occupies that space now. Above, where the owners of the store once kept grain, there's a large room with a sunken bathtub.

The rest of the rooms are but lightly restored from the old inn. John seems as fascinated by the history here as we are. Recently, the niece of an early innkeeper returned for a visit, adding to John's stock of stories. "She told me that when the ferry could not go, because the reach was iced over, islanders would drive across the reach," he says. "But because the ice was saltwater, it was loose—you know, almost spongy. This woman said she could remember the ice swaying beneath the car and her uncle gunning the motor, going as quick as he could to get over the ice."

Another part of the Deer Isle economy is craftspeople. Many came to attend a session at the Haystack Mountain School of Crafts, farther down on the island, and never left. Signs here and throughout the island lead to the home studios of weavers, potters, and other makers who welcome visitors. Galleries in Deer Isle and Stonington frequently display their work.

One craftswoman, Kathy Woell, who turns her woven cloth into clothing, can be found down this short road.

Back on State 15 are more craftspeople, including George Hardy, one of the state's prominent folk carvers. He works in the woodshed behind his home, just at State 15, and sells his humorous wooden animals, whirligigs, and Noah's arks directly from the shed.

Now we head down State 15, toward Stonington. The village of Deer Isle winds around a center common. There's a little historical society in a building being restored with community help.

Having passed up fish and chips on Caterpillar Hill, we are hungry and decide to lunch in Stonington. Were we not hungry, we might have taken Reach Road from near Ferry Road, following the north coast, or the left turn just outside Deer Isle village which leads to Haystack Mountain School of Crafts, a world-renowned craft school where professionals and amateurs come together for sessions of from one to three weeks throughout the summer. People blow glass, throw pots, forge iron, make paper, hammer jewelry, weave, and work in a dozen other crafts. The place not only creates beauty, it is beauty, worth a visit for the architecture alone, though frequently there are also lectures, entertainment, and exhibits open to the public. The school has recently instituted a weekly tour for visitors.

On cream-colored cliffs cascading to Jericho Bay, off Penobscot Bay, rows of weathered gray cottages descend to the bay, centered by a staircase that both anchors and frames tree, land, and school. Designed by architect Edward Larrabee Barnes, Haystack won a prestigious architectural award when it was first built. In 1994, it won a twenty-five-year repeat of the award—the place still astounds.

Haystack is located on Stinson Neck off the village called Sunshine. (Deer Isle has a Sunset, too, on its western shore.) Signs direct visitors there at a point in the road known as the Haulover, where Deer Isle is pinched to almost nothing. Native Americans and later settlers hauled their canoes over the land to get to the water on the other side.

Stonington is about five miles down State 15. Almost there, at the moment where State 15 plummets toward town, we bear left toward the pink water lilies of Ames Pond, then turn around, famished, to drive down the major section of Main Street and up Opera House Hill for a fried-fish lunch at Fisherman's Friend. There are other restaurants in town, however, at least two right on Main Street, as well as a gourmet grocery store.

I am always amazed at how much of Stonington there is. Unlike many New England towns, it is not centered around a common, but focused on the water. The main drag has at least three sections of waterfront road, and where Main Street stays inland, there are roads leading out to the Deer Island

Thorofare. The quarries and great fisheries brought a mixture of people here, then the quarries closed and the fisheries slowed, leaving an impatience for something else. It's frequently an audible impatience: cars screech and roar, take tight turns, and stop on a dime.

This is the place to splurge on an excursion trip, on the Isle au Haut ferry, or on a kayak rental. Merchant's Row, a scattering of islands beyond the thorofare, is named not for a mythical row of merchant ships waiting their turn to unload their cargo at Stonington (as I assumed), but for Merchant Island, which was named after a Mr. Merchant. It is an exquisite spot. The Maine mixture of rock and fir and water is squeezed to the most beautiful edge by the pink granite. The rocks are just beneath the surface, so the light bounces off them, giving the waters a tropical, green-blue hue.

And from off the coast I can best appreciate one of Maine's great sights: the large, wooden, green opera house standing on a bluff in the center of town, its name, "OPERA HOUSE," advertised to all in large white letters. Though the building is not open on a regular schedule, there are still summer entertainment and movies there.

A lot of exploring is possible in this town of Victorian homes and spectacular vistas. For the briefest of detours, we take the causeway to Moose Island, passing a major lobster pound and Billings Marine, the chief marine garage this side of Camden, servicing lobster boats and yachts alike, the Rockefellers' boats among them.

As we head back north via the western shore, West Main Street becomes Sand Beach Road, clinging close to the coast. Soon we can see the thick beams and cranes of Crotch Island quarry, which is once again in service. The granite industry, so important to the state for fifty or more years after the Civil War, foundered after the proliferation of skyscrapers. Most Maine quarries are now deep pools of water. Crotch Island, with its pink granite, reopened to a new process. The granite is taken in blocks, but frequently sliced into thin sheets and used as facing material. Thicker polished granite is also now sought for kitchen counters and tables.

For medium-strength bikers like myself, there are several possible bicycle loops here, allowing an even slower pace than back-road driving.

At West Stonington, at the tip of the harbor known as Burnt Cove, we link up with the road to Sunset, but only briefly, for we now bear left for Crockett Cove, a deep wood so blessed by fog and rain that it has become a coastal "fog forest," with a floor of pine needles and soft moss. Take a map at the box; we didn't and found ourselves back on the road. This beautiful, old-growth woods, with its many species of moss, was given to the Nature Conservancy by Emily Muir, a dauntless artist and architect. In the summer of 1994 she placed small figures of Stonington people in galleries throughout the island, pursuing yet another medium, though she's well into her nineties.

Returning from Crockett Cove we turn down the next road, toward Goose Cove Lodge at Stinson Point (not to be confused with Stinson Neck, on the eastern side of the island). We drive past the cottages associated with the lodge and enter the main building to find a thin woman, hair covered by a deep hat, gently placing large mushrooms into a small basket. She has been collecting mushrooms all her life, she explains to us, interrupting instructions she's giving to the lodge's host on how to prepare these particular ones. She shows us the speckled top of an amanita mushroom she found, one of the two amanitas that are edible. With her eyes bathed in mascara and her absolute directness, this mushroom-loving biologist reminds me of Louise Nevelson, raised due west of here as the ship sails, in that other granite-quarrying town, Rockland (see Chapter 4).

The lodge fronts on Goose Cove, which leads out to Barred Island (one of several islands in the bay by that name, which refers not to thorny foliage but to its sandbar). The modern, cozy lodge dining room has a wide vista overlooking the cove. Behind the dining room is a most comfortable sitting room with a small bar and a large library offering a wide range of books.

Those longing for the water might well decide to stay here, for kayaks, canoes, and rowboats are offered to guests, and a walk out to Barred Island, given the right timing (the island is reachable by land only when the tide is low), approximates the special isolation of the islands farther out in Penobscot Bay.

Other trails also lead from the spot where there's a sign posted "Parking for Barred Island." Detailed guides to these trails, available at the lodge, speak of the birds, the mosses, and the change of air within the woods.

As I walk on the beach, worrying a rose hip in my fingers, I wonder at the beauty of this bay. It has been the source of inspiration for many. John Marin painted these islands and lands, as did Fairfield Porter. Marin worked here for about thirteen years before moving farther down east to Cape Split, off Addison, in 1933. Porter summered in Penobscot Bay, on Great Spruce Head Island due west of Deer Isle, from 1912 until his death in 1985. Porter's brother, Eliot, photographed the island, producing the greatly heralded book *Summer Island*. Buckminster Fuller also owned an island in the bay, Bear Island. To admire his island, he bought a house in Sunset, on a bluff near a golf course, overlooking the bay.

We continue on the road past Sunset and through Deer Isle village, where the imposing Pilgrim's Inn is a mecca for many guests, either for dinner or lodging. We make a brief stop at the Turtle Gallery, run by artist Elena Kubler. The current show is mostly crafts: decorated hand puppets, hammered silver children's cups and spoons by Elena, large woven rugs by Sarah Hotchkiss, beautifully colored drawings of fruit by our friend artist Majo Keleshian, and animated prints by Susan Webster.

We now leave the island, returning north, relishing again the Deer Isle causeway and the bridge spanning Eggemoggin Reach. On the right just over the bridge is Wayward Books, offering what part-owner Sybil Pike calls "choice used and medium rare books."

A left at Sargentville on State 15/State 175 is a quick escape back up the peninsula. But we drive straight, through Sargentville, on State 175, delighting in the Victorian-style Sargentville Chapel and the tiny post office, located in a farmhouse. Nearing Sedgwick, with its brightly painted houses of yellow and blue, we pass some formal herb gardens on our left.

We now cross the Benjamin River, where at low tide we see the remnants of two dams. We are in Brooklin, so named because a brook, the Benjamin River, is the town line—brook-line. Among the white houses coiffed in purple wisteria is a tree house built like a yacht for some lucky child. Soon, we pass the real thing, large green buildings and a sign for Duffy & Duffy Yachts, where lobster boats as well as fiberglass yachts are built. Sharon, at the yard, says they are quite happy to show people how shipbuilding is done.

Duffy & Duffy are among some four or even more boatbuilders in the broad township of Brooklin. In Center Harbor, down the road, Joel White, son of E. B. White, builds and restores wooden boats, populating the harbor with his own handsome designs.

But just before we get there, we take a short detour through the summer colony known as Haven, the setting for *Colony,* a popular novel published in 1992 by summer resident

*The Brooklin General Store opens at 5:30 A.M.
and closes after dark*

Anne Rivers Siddons. Here, beyond tall rosebushes, stand old clusters of cottages centered around a yacht club, calling forth a life of summer ease.

Center Harbor is a short drive off State 175. We take a right at the Island Winds studio and gallery (a mansard-roofed building at the corner). As we come to the harbor, the sky suddenly grays, casting a slanting light over the water. The light reminds me of the paintings of Edward Hopper, another artist who feasted on the beauties of the Maine coast.

Perhaps we've made enough detours. But now Bill's at the wheel and just before the village of Brooklin he turns right for a drive down Naskeag Point, unable to resist another boating spot. Here is where *WoodenBoat* magazine is produced and where the WoodenBoat School offers summertime workshops in the art of wooden boatbuilding. The school is housed in an old mansion, the offices located in the small upstairs rooms originally built for maids, butlers, and other servants. Visitors are welcome, though the school is not open weekends. On the first weekend in August (the same weekend that the state's big art festival, the Maine Festival, is held in southern Maine), there's an international regatta of wooden boats leaving from the point. It's a festival of sails, classic and modern, schooner and skiff, creating a confusion of canvas and wood and water that perhaps approximates the view seen everywhere along this coast only a hundred years ago.

Back again in the twentieth century and on State 175, we drive by the petite Brooklin Library and the Morning Moon Cafe (a fine place to stop for coffee, dessert, or a meal). Out of town on our right is a two-story white clapboard farmhouse, set not too far back from the road, in a field dotted with flowers and heading to the sea. This was the home of Katherine and E. B. White.

Soon after, the road enters a close wood with alluring driveways to houses we can only guess at. As in other towns along this coast, there are also many "For Sale" signs. Those who wish to stop for a lifetime could settle in.

When the view opens up again, we've rounded the eastern corner of the Blue Hill peninsula. The vista is no longer the Camden Hills to the west or Isle au Haut to the south, but across Blue Hill Bay to Mount Desert Island.

As we approach South Blue Hill, we pass a large chicken barn on our left with a sign announcing One New World Plaza. This is the home of WERU, a wide-ranging community radio station. WERU is in Blue Hill Falls because Noel Paul Stookey (of Peter, Paul, and Mary) created studio space in the henhouse. In the late 1980s, Stookey offered to help launch a community radio station in the ground-floor studios with initial financing through his foundation, Public Domain. Musician Paul Sullivan also has studio space in the building. It's a station of volunteers that welcomes visitors.

Beyond the station, passing large farmhouses surrounded by equally large porches conveying an old-world sense of settled comfort, the road leads down a short, steep hill to a concrete bridge over Blue Hill Falls. If cars are lining the road, and kayakers and canoeists are plying the waters below, then the tide is right for the fourth, broadest, and most popular of the region's reversing falls, offering the fun of almost endless whitewater, at least until the tide goes slack, without the worry of hidden rocks.

I love these falls. But even more, I love the view we are now approaching, when for a moment the road leads down to the rocky shoreline, revealing a spot where forest, rock, and ocean are held in perfect, breathtaking balance.

The town of Blue Hill sits just north of here, a right turn at the crossroads by the IGA, onto State 15/State 176.

The draw of Blue Hill is not new. Thousands of years ago, the elusive Native American tribe known as the Red Paint

People came to bury the ocher-covered bodies of their dead near Blue Hills Falls. Shortly after the American Revolution, Jonathan Fisher came. He was parson to a parish of shipbuilders and fishing folk, a missionary to the Native Americans, and a man who designed and built a good portion of his own house, filled it with furniture he created, and set his own handcrafted clock into the chimney. He wrote books of poetry and natural history, farmed his land, and rather sternly preached the good book. He was also an artist whose acclaim has grown with the centuries. His painting *Morning in Blue Hill*, part of the Farnsworth's permanent collection (see Chapter 4), is a joy for its simple directness.

Fisher's house, open seasonally, would be a left turn at the intersection of State 15/State 176.

The town of Blue Hill has excellent restaurants, a modern-day music cafe at the Left Bank, galleries, walks, a highly acclaimed chamber music school and an excellent winter chamber music series, a classic state fair, and the height of land called Blue Hill. To find the trailhead, follow State 172 north, then turn left as the fairgrounds appear on the right. The trailhead is up the hill on the right.

The fairgrounds are most active over Labor Day. This is a wild, typically earthy fair, with lots of rides, thick hot dogs, horse-pulling contests, racing-car stunt drivers, plenty of animals, and plenty of crowds.

In late June, we park to visit the town's two bookstores and the Handworks Gallery, a cheery space filled with brightly colored crafts. At the corner of Parker Point Road, the Blue Hill Library has old murals, while down the road, the Judith Leighton Gallery offers art that tends toward the joyful—landscapes and whimsical scenes with a metaphysical edge. Her sculpture garden grows fuller and more complex by the year.

Marsden Hartley spoke of the "deep, rich solitude" of this area. When visiting in high summer, it is sometimes hard to find much solitude in town, but a walk down this road, through the golf course to some stones reaching into the harbor, and Hartley's solitude sings. Come lonely winter, when solitude whispers in every moist streetlight, I've found quite welcome camaraderie here, along with ringing peals of laughter, sledding down the golf course's well-traveled hills.

In the Area

Cold Comfort Productions, Castine, 207-326-9041.

Compass Rose Books, Castine, 207-326-9366.

Maine Maritime Academy, Castine, 207-326-4311.

Wilson Museum, Castine, 207-326-8753.

Bah's Bakehouse, Castine, 207-326-9510.

Dennett's Wharf, Castine, 207-326-9045.

Castine Inn, Castine, 207-326-4365.

The Manor, Castine, 207-326-4861.

Holiday House, Castine, 207-326-4335.

Pentagoet Inn, Castine, 207-326-8616.

Village Inn, Castine, 207-326-9366.

Larson Gallery, South Penobscot, 207-326-8222.

North Country Textiles, South Penobscot, 207-326-4131.

The Real Thing! South Penobscot.

Northern Bay Market, South Penobscot, 207-326-8606.

Holbrook Island Sanctuary, Cape Rosier, 207-326-4012.

Metinic Yacht Corporation, Horseshoe Cove, Cape Rosier, 207-326-4411.

Bagaduce Chorale, Brooksville, 207-326-8532.

Buck's Harbor Yacht Club, Brooksville, 207-326-8839.

Country View Restaurant, Sedgwick, 207-359-2214.

Eggemoggin Inn, Deer Isle, 207-348-2540.

Deer Isle Artists Association, Deer Isle, 207-348-9955.

George Hardy, carvings, Deer Isle, 207-348-2885.

Haystack Mountain School of Crafts, Deer Isle, 207-348-2306.

Turtle Gallery, Deer Isle, 207-348-9977.

Kathy Woell, weaver, Deer Isle.

Goose Cove Lodge, Deer Isle, 207-348-2508.

Inn at Ferry Landing, Deer Isle, 207-348-7760.

Pilgrim's Inn, Deer Isle, 207-348-6615.

Eastern Bay Cooperative Gallery, Stonington, 207-367-5006.

New England Stone Industries, Inc., Crotch Island, Stonington, 207-367-2735.

Palmer Day IV, Stonington, 207-367-2207.

Fisherman's Friend, Stonington, 207-367-2442.

Wayward Books, Sargentville, 207-359-2397.

Duffy & Duffy Yachts, Brooklin, 207-359-4658.

Island Winds Gallery, Brooklin, 207-359-2714.

WoodenBoat School, Brooklin, 207-359-4651.

Morning Moon Cafe, Brooklin, 207-359-2373.

WERU, Blue Hills Falls, 207-374-2313.

Bagaduce Music Lending Library, Blue Hill, 207-374-5454.

Blue Hill Concert Association, Blue Hill, 207-374-2161.

Blue Hill Fair, Blue Hill, Labor Day weekend.

Blue Hill Public Library, Blue Hill, 207-374-5515.

Jonathan Fisher Memorial, Blue Hill, 207-374-2459.

Handworks Gallery, Blue Hill, 207-374-5613.

Kneisel Hall, Blue Hill, 207-374-2811.

Judith Leighton Gallery, Blue Hill, 207-374-5501.

Rackliffe Pottery Inc., Blue Hill, 207-374-2297.

Rowantrees Pottery, Blue Hill, 207-374-5535.

Firepond, Blue Hill, 207-374-2131.

Jonathan's, Blue Hill, 207-374-5226.

The Left Bank Cafe, Blue Hill, 207-374-2201.

Pie in the Sky, Blue Hill, 207-374-5570.

Blue Hill Inn, Blue Hill, 207-374-2844.

Surry Opera Company, Surry, 207-667-2629.

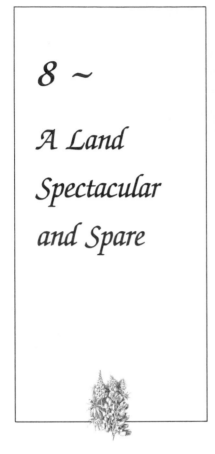

8 ~

A Land

Spectacular

and Spare

Getting there: From southern Maine, take I-95 to Augusta, then take State 3 to Belfast and US 1/State 3 north to Ellsworth.

Highlights: *Wreath making and Christmas tree farms; the historic Thomas Ruggles House; the Jonesport Lobster Boat Races; hiking on Great Wass Island; historic Machias; Passamaquoddy Indian woven baskets; fishing villages of Eastport and Lubec; Pembroke's Reversing Falls Park; and West Quoddy Head Light, the easternmost point in the United States.*

Traveling down east takes us to land both spectacular and spare. This is the farthest edge of Maine's rocky coast, where entire stretches of land seem almost overlooked. Houses are abandoned, doorways left to run wild with pink roses, cars overgrown with daisies. Not that no one lives here, but fewer do than in earlier days.

Eastport is the final destination on this trip I take with Daniel. It is less than three hours from Ellsworth, our starting point, but I spend two days, edging the coast around Jonesport, returning via Cutler. Those wishing to explore nature trails, linger in historic museums, or take a boat through coastal islands might consider three days, perhaps more.

We begin in late June, leaving from Ellsworth along US 1. To get here from southern Maine, we again have the choice of taking I-95 to Augusta and State 3 to Belfast, joining with US 1/State 3 north to Ellsworth, or taking I-95 to Bangor, exiting onto I-395 and taking US 1A to Ellsworth.

Ellsworth is our frontier supply stop. We join people from the entire region—Blue Hill and Mount Desert Island, Jonesport and Machias—who come to fortify themselves with worldly goods. The twentieth century is well established in Ellsworth, displacing solid nineteenth-century elegance.

In a small mall, Daniel races me to some rides: a jet plane and a three-seater merry-go-round. When I drag him away from this pleasure palace, he is so sleepy that he doesn't see the McDonald's yellow *M* near the turnoff for US 1, which veers left from State 3. It's easy to miss this turn, since the bulk of the traffic continues on State 3 to Mount Desert Island.

It isn't until we take that turn onto US 1 that I feel we have begun our journey. We follow US 1 for only about four miles, then turn left again at State 182 direct to Cherryfield, a forested back road, quicker than US 1.

As we pass West Franklin and the turnoffs for State 200, I think of the way people, like rocks, get sifted over the globe. Living in Eastbrook, population 262, is a painter named Paul Alexandre John, raised in India, of Armenian heritage, and married to a patrician Philadelphian. John's elaborate, colorful canvases peppered with quizzically smiling figures can be seen around Ellsworth, or at the Judith Leighton Gallery in Blue Hill (see Chapter 7).

On State 182, we stop at a yard sale, one of the semipermanent kind. That people spend lots of time trading broken, used goods could be one sign of a depression. To keep these continual yard sales going, the sellers comb other yard sales, as well as trash piles and dumps (though most dumps already have their own "yard" sale, the attendant swiftly making a trash triage between car and compactor—very little actually gets trashed). The goods grow dirtier through the summer as the items absorb road dust and rain. For 75 cents (reduced from $1.00), I buy an inch-long plastic car driven by Pluto that began life as a McDonald's giveaway.

Soon after, we leave the town of Franklin—billing itself as the Christmas Tree Capital of the World—and move into a place known only as TR 94, as if to confirm my feeling of pushing into a spare land, bared even of a name.

But of course it's not barren. We are in lush woods, passing an overhanging oak grove and Tunk Lake, where there's a tiny pulloff with a boat ramp and a boulder large enough for a carside picnic. With the help of the state's Land for Maine's Future program, 14,000 acres of this dense forest with its extensive lakes were recently given over to the public.

This forested portion ends abruptly at the Narraguagus (Na-ra-GWAY-gus) River and Cherryfield, the first of three stalwart down-east river towns above Pleasant Bay through which we will be passing. Like so many coastal towns, these achieved prosperity with the related nineteenth-century industries of lumbering and shipbuilding.

One hundred years ago, Cherryfield bustled with a multitude of industries—gristmill; planing mill; sash, door, and blind factory; foundry and machine shop; gang saw; edge and lath mill—a reminder of how self-sufficient towns were, regardless of how elaborate life was. Shoes, furniture, clothing, and carriages were also made here, but those were the staples. Cherryfield was mostly associated with shipbuilding and seafaring. When lumber traveled by river, the Narraguagus artery between Cherryfield and Milbridge, located about 5.5 miles downstream, was crucial.

Much of Cherryfield—175 acres on both sides of the river—is a historic district. As we drive through, I understand why. The houses are imposing and varied, a lesson in nineteenth-century architectural styles, and a reminder of former prosperity, including Federal, Greek Revival, Italianate, Queen Anne, Colonial Revival, and Second Empire homes. They represent the extended era when Cherryfield prevailed in the thick of the commercial world.

Recently, I saw a six-minute home movie made in Cherryfield in 1938, one of many great archival films collected at Northeast Historic Film (see Chapter 6). This is both a glimpse of old Cherryfield and a record of how unfamiliar the motion camera once was. How do you pose for a movie camera? you can hear people wondering aloud as they fidget, uncomfortably, standing stock-still, and looking very, vulnerably, human. Just about everyone in town is asked to do so—grocery store clerk, gas station attendant, students from the Cherryfield Academy. All but a few—a baby bundled in its carriage, a farmhand asleep on a hay wagon, and the town's star horse racer—look clearly embarrassed.

Today, Cherryfield is known as the "Blueberry Capital of the World," primarily for its two processing plants at the north end of town.

We see early signs of the coming harvest in the form of notices advertising for blueberry workers. As many as 8,000 people are needed to bring in the crop, which is still raked by hand using a deep dustpan-like box edged with teeth. The season lasts from four to six weeks, with August in the middle. People flock from all over to join the harvest: Native Americans from Canada and the Maine reservations work here as part of their traditional round of seasonal activity; students earn college tuition or spending money; local people depend on it; and recently, even migrants from Mexico and the Southwest have made their way here. Earnings average about $4,000 for the four to six weeks, with a good raker pulling in much more.

After the harvest is done, hundreds are needed to process the berries, which can be canned, frozen, or liquefied. Maine produces about half the wild blueberries in the nation,

Blueberry rakers harvest Maine's wild blueberries

and about one-fifth of the cultivated (or high-bush) blue-berries. Wild blues are the ones we see throughout this part of Maine, a rusty groundcover in fall, a white flower in spring, if it has not been burned. Wild means anything from farmers who simply burn half the crop each year to enhance the strength of the plant to those who dig irrigation ditches with fertilizer flowing through.

We briefly drive upriver, following signs for shore access, and find that the road leads us alongside Cherryfield Foods, one of the two large blueberry processing plants in town. Jasper Wyman and Sons is just beyond. Wyman is one of the oldest growers in the state (it was founded in 1874), and probably the largest, but it doesn't like to admit it.

It's Saturday and the plants are closed, so we keep to our course, which is to drive past the dam's erector-set construction of beams and gears to a small, quiet riverside park before returning downriver to where State 182 joins US 1.

Shortly after turning left onto US 1, I stop for a moment at the Mill River Antique and Salvage Shop on the east side of the road, fronted by a yard of bikes, stoves, hubcaps, carved wooden bears, and genuinely fascinating clutter. The owner, Jerry Blackburn, is also collecting items for a Downeast Museum of Natural History and Art, which he hopes to establish somewhere in Washington County. That's the future. The present is a shop to get lost in, especially with a sign stating: "Prices are not firm."

The road narrows as we head for Harrington, five miles up the road, passing more old houses, fading lupine fields, a couple of antique and gift shops, and several Victorian buildings, as well as roadsides thick with Indian paintbrush, buttercups, and clover spreading orange, yellow, and lavender across the fields. The washes of color change weekly in summer. Last week it was lupines. Later on it will be purple vetch, and perhaps wild roses. And always, there are blueberries.

Harrington comes alive in December, when the wreath season is in full swing. Worcester Wreaths, located in an old school here, is one of the largest producers of wreaths in the state. As many as three million wreaths are made in the state by individuals and small factories.

Leaving Harrington en route to Columbia Falls, we pass more antique stores, a place selling plastic paddleboats, and a Baptist church with brown shingles, quite lovely. Like most of these coastal towns, Harrington once thrived on shipbuilding.

When I turn right off US 1 at the sign for the Thomas Ruggles House, I find a quiet road with no noise, no sign of people, though as we drive near the small falls from which the town gets its name, a silver-colored car moves off from the grassy lot and out onto the highway. Behind us is the Ruggles House, one of New England's architectural treasures, built subtly, with a delicate perfection. Even the exterior woodwork is engaging, with ribbons and hearts over the windows, turning wood into fabric. Over the porch, the wood looks more like pieces of wrought iron. Ruggles made his fortune in lumber. In 1818, he had this copiously detailed home with a soaring staircase built for him, his wife, and nine children. In 1820, he died. His family grew poorer by the year, though they held onto the place. Legend has it that an Englishman was imprisoned here for three years until he finished carving the woodwork with a penknife. The carpenter has been fairly certainly identified as Alvah Peterson, an itinerant carver who traveled the countryside, working on people's homes. He spent about a year in the Ruggles home and also carved in some other nearby houses.

Arthur Train, a popular early-twentieth-century writer who summered on Mount Desert Island, set his story *The House that Tutt Built* here. Later, Train was instrumental in raising money to restore the home, which had fallen into great disrepair. Its final owners, two unmarried Ruggles granddaughters, sold off pieces of family silver and antique furniture to live. Neighbors used to help out by leaving firewood and food at their doorstep. Even so, it may have been malnutrition that ended the elderly life of Elizabeth, the last granddaughter.

Leaving the home, I pay a quick visit to the Columbia Falls Pottery down the road, and then walk back to the Pleasant River. On a ridge across US 1 stand more nineteenth-century homes and one stalwart eighteenth-century one. Though it's only June, the afternoon heat is as dry as the straw under my feet, brittle as the bones of the late Elizabeth Ruggles.

We spend barely a minute back on US 1 before turning down State 187 toward Jonesport. The road winds over and around gentle hills, the drought-dry grass bleached to butter yellow. Sheets hang in the wind from a line attached to the peeling white boards of a lone farmhouse. Nearby, there's a trailer home. It's either farmhouses or trailers on this route. Though Jonesport is a center of activity and economy as Columbia Falls was once, producing 3.5 million feet of lumber annually, in addition to ships, State 187 seems so lonely that I find myself wondering what the few who live here do, where they work, how far they must travel, what brought them to this lonely edge of the sea.

When Jonesport was but a small fishing village in the nineteenth century, Indian River was the cultural center.

From there, in 1866, a group of twenty families left for Jaffa, in Palestine. The great-great-grandfather of Jonesport's current first selectman, Keith Church, was a young boy at the time, and the memory has lasted. The group of Mainers endured four years of trouble in the arid climate, then the bulk of them returned, in disgrace.

"My family was so ashamed they wouldn't talk about it for 100 years," says Church. But now he's talking about it. The leader, he says, was a charmer, an "excommunicated Mormon charlatan, an entrepreneur trying to build an empire." Church recalls his grandfather describing him as having "eyes so close together, they could look down the neck of a vinegar bottle."

Some of the group died, some just suffered the loss of their incomes. Mark Twain somehow got involved and paid the return passage for Church's family. But some stayed. Church says they are there today, running a large trucking company and a good travel agency.

This story reminds me that back up in Addison, due south of Columbia Falls, Dino Fonda has been working since 1991 on a sixty-five-foot schooner to sail to the Holy Land. As of 1994, the ship's stalwart ribs were still showing, yet it had the bulk and weight of Noah's ark. But Fonda is not trying to hoodwink anyone else into the activity. "It's just the Lord and I," building the ship, he says.

We continue driving beside the Indian River. Glimpses of rock crevices and sentinel-like houses appear. Though we're moving south to Jonesport, the road sign reads "State 187 north."

The river erodes my sense of desolation as it broadens to look more like a bay or an inlet as it approaches Moosabec Reach. After a short distance, we come to thriving Jonesport.

But as frequently happens in rural Maine, I feel as if I've driven not to another place but to another decade, the 1940s perhaps. We pass a few junkyards and trailer homes, the trailers so old-fashioned that they look as if they were truly meant to be attached to a car.

Now we've arrived in West Jonesport. With its rows of clapboard homes painted a multitude of colors, and its street signs carved into the shape of lobster boats, this is a town of endless charm. Like Jonesport and Beals Island, this is a working town, a lobstering town. For some reason, I am drawn to the homes painted a thick mustard yellow.

We turn right to drive through West Jonesport, passing a young girl pushing a child in a stroller. She stops to pick deep-blue irises growing wild in a ditch by the side of the road. A duck and five ducklings march across the road. I wait, then drive to the end of the line, a lobster wharf.

I am fascinated by this pretty town, with its houses encased by summer's flowers—the entire cycle blooming together—wild pink roses cascading by the roadside and walls of lilacs against the houses. Even the lupines, which have faded farther south, still retain their rich color and stately stature. Summer erupts here with fierce swiftness. There is not much time.

This is no summer colony, but the town has the feeling of a haven. At a nearby church, balloons surround a sign announcing the birth of Michelle Lee.

Turning back from West Jonesport, I take a right over the bridge to Beals Island.

Every July 4th, this steeply arching span, which is not quite tall enough for a mast to sail under (forcing sailors to take the long way around), becomes a vantage point for watching the Jonesport Lobster Boat Races. The boats rev up, sporting raucous and flagrantly politically incorrect names such as *Benny's Bitch*, then zoom under the bridge, racing in pairs. For the uninitiated—us, the year we saw it—it seemed something of a nonevent. There were so many pairs of boats that no one seemed too interested in the eliminations. Gossip was the main activity on the bridge. But every so often, the crowd would get taken in by the bravado of one or another racer. We found that the hubbub around the races, the mild commotion, the hot dogs and soda, were all great fun, a coastal family event, a big deal for lobstermen who attend from around the coast, and an even bigger deal for the boatbuilders—an obvious fact that nevertheless failed to come to me until much later. A winning boat is a boon to its builder.

There's a lot to explore on Beals Island and the connecting Great Wass Island. We could easily spend a full weekend here, in which case we would take a long walk through The Nature Conservancy preserve that covers at least two-thirds of Great Wass Island, and also contact Capt. Barna Norton. He leads trips to Machias Seal Island, ten miles out to sea, where, in summer, puffins nest among razorbills and terns.

A left turn over the bridge takes us to Beals. On our way we pass lobster shacks, several boatbuilders, and a little seaside cemetery studded with decorations—pink, red, green, and orange flowers arranged in small crocks. The bright, almost garish colors bring me back to Mexico, with its mesmerizing celebrations of death, and seem a bit unusual for eastern Maine.

After the causeway, we take a right for Great Wass. Before going to the nature preserve, I first drive the dirt road as far as I can, passing some rental cottages at Norton Point, turning around at the sign announcing "Road Ends Here," as if it were the name of a place. (The roads beyond are private, and explorations are discouraged.) A home over the bay has nearly a dozen birdhouses on its lawn, perched along tall poles—a skyscraper city of the birds. We are almost at open ocean here, almost at the end of the world.

About halfway back through the island, on the east side of the road, I find the parking lot for hikers headed into the preserve. Just beyond is a lobster pound by the shore and a duck pond on the island side, a bit off the road.

Because the island is so foggy and wet, almost touching the open ocean, the climate here is cold. This preserve is actually an outpost of the subarctic zone, with deep bogs covered by shrubs, moss, and berries, and large stands of gnarled jack pines. For a time, the trail passes along a deep and beautiful fjord, known rather incongruously as the Mud Hole. The full loop is five miles—a five-hour trip—and it can be wet.

A Land Spectacular and Spare

This is one of Maine's enchanted lands. One beach is composed of flat slabs of pink granite, looking as if pale whales had been beached there. Some beaches are unusually sandy; others are covered by boulders. Another beach looks as if it were made entirely of driftwood, only the wood did not drift. The trees there had long since died, leaving sinuous ghost forms. Off the coast, at low tide, seals sun on the exposed rocks.

But don't go expecting views. This is fog land. I've come here when it was clear on US 1 and so foggy here we could barely see beyond the steering wheel, never mind the seals. But I've also found a special intimacy in the fog. As The Nature Conservancy's guide *Maine Forever* explains, this is the essence of the region: "The wild, windswept islands of the Great Wass archipelago are especially memorable on a still foggy morning. . . . The fog eddies over bare ledges through the twisted, dark forms of jack pines [while] down on the shore, the mists ebb and flow, softening the pink of the granite ledges and turning the sea a platinum blue."

Returning back across Moosabec Reach, I drive slowly, reluctant to leave the gentle wind and intimate, moist air, so much like Maine's coastal islands. And of course, it is an island, linked only by this crescent of a bridge.

Across State 187 from the bridge stands Tall Barney's Restaurant, a local gathering place, announced by a man in his undershirt toting a large suitcase under each arm. Inside there are papers stacked for customers to read and a long central table reserved for lobstermen.

We turn right on State 187 at a closed-down clothing store with a wonderful sign featuring a huge fisherman sporting even larger foul-weather overalls. We're in Jonesport proper, with well-painted houses, a new church under construction, and a passion for basketball. Winter high-school games rival

173

the summer lobster-boat contests as essential community activities.

On State 187 toward Jonesboro, the houses still seem prosperous. After moving inland along an extensive peat bog, the road now nears the shore, where stretches of grass plunge to Englishman Bay. Soon the road moves inland again, winding through mowed fields and past large farmhouses bleeding fist-sized flecks of paint reminiscent of Andrew Wyeth's *Christina's World* (see Chapter 4). These houses sit in their yellow-green fields that lead to vast, astounding vistas that scrub the visitor's soul.

Suddenly, I feel as if I've crossed a line, shedding the present, eliminating the baroque busyness of life, with all its plastic toys and worldly focus on *things*—all that gets in the way of each day. Oddly, because I live partway to this place, I have to come all the way to here to get to this point of awareness. Others might find it enough to journey only as far as where I already live.

Back on US 1, beyond Jonesboro, with its turret-topped Union Church, these hours suddenly feel enchanted. Now there is a resoluteness to the road, a single-minded pursuit of the future.

We head to Machias, past a ridge from which the county spreads out, barrens and rocks, lakes and nubbled trees. There is a moment before descending into Machias when this small town emerges in a cacophony of pale colors and muted shapes. Below is the rushing ribbon of the town's waterfalls— those "bad little falls" that give the town its name. Beyond lie the smoothly rounded hills, with the spires of the courthouse and the Congregational and Catholic churches pricking the watery wash of blue and white sky.

That geographic instant is recalled in the painting *Machias, Maine*, by John Marin, who spent his last years east of here, at the tip of the Addison peninsula. The watercolor hangs at the University of Maine at Machias, one of many gifts to the town from the Marin family. Another of the gifts— the Marin Foundation Collection of fifteen paintings by Marin and such friends as Lyonel Feininger and William Kienbusch—is in the permanent collection of the Powers Hall Gallery of the university, thanks to Norma Marin, daughter-in-law of the artist and a fierce believer in the arts.

Machias, however, may best be known for its Revolutionary War history. In early May 1775, the *Margaretta*, an armed British vessel, arrived in Machias, demanding some lumber for the British barracks in Boston. The Machias folk, loath to arm their enemy, erected a liberty pole and launched an attack that captured the *Margaretta* and inscribed Machias as the site of the first naval battle of the Revolution. That night, Hannah Weston, a Jonesboro woman, traveled for hours to bring powder to the rebels so they could achieve their ends.

Most of this action occurred in Machiasport, which can be reached by driving down State 92. The Gates House there is open to visitors.

Also open is Burnham Tavern, a pale-yellow building on High and Free Streets in Machias, where the attack was first planned and where the wounded were delivered. The British captain died at the tavern, but several of his soldiers were nursed back to health. The tavern is now a museum, the oldest building east of the Penobscot River.

Machias seems to take its falls for granted. Though there is a park on the other side of the river leading to a bridge across the falls, on the Main Street side only the parking lots face the falls. The water inevitably draws me, even when winter's chill turns it into a silent image of frozen motion. In midspring, I've seen an array of nets draped over the waters, as if performing an ancient ritual; but this is no ritual, only smelt, which run here in mid-May. Completing the ancient picture, cormorants rest on the rocks, shaking their wings wide like black phantoms. Sometimes even seals can be seen here, having swum up the Machias River from Machias Bay.

There's more to town, including a well-stocked five-and-ten and a theater company working out of a not-quite-makeshift second-story theater on the main street. This weekend, we find that a small traveling carnival has settled itself on the other edge of town. I promise Daniel we'll return. We have places to go, today, people to see, and it is getting to be late afternoon.

Leaving town, we pass Helen's Restaurant, famous for its strawberry pie—as well as its pies of rhubarb, strawberry-rhubarb, raspberry, blueberry, apple, chocolate cream, butterscotch, lemon meringue, peanut butter, and more.

Machias lingers on through East Machias, where the Riverside Inn, on the river, seems situated to provide water views from almost every window.

But I've reached my limit for what I can take in. We are but an hour from Eastport, so I give Daniel a new green lollypop and we head north on US 1 among daisies, Indian paintbrush, and wild, wet irises, with intermittent lakes and bogs beyond. I want to arrive in Eastport with some time to hunt for our lodgings, and we're expected at a 7:00 P.M. dance recital.

Near Cobscook Bay, we pass a long bridge over some wetlands. The state park here offers campsites right on the water—at least at high tide. We're entering into a channel of deep tidal changes, where the water rushes out twenty feet from the shore. Bring bug protection, if you're going to camp. My one stay here was as memorable for bugs as for views.

About eleven miles beyond the state park, we pass Pembroke, where we will return to see the spectacular reversing falls at the end of this peninsula. We now see signs for freshly smoked salmon. Salmon hatcheries have become a new and rather strong industry around Eastport.

Then comes Perry, advertising itself as the halfway point between the North Pole and the equator, so we must be due east of Doc Grant's restaurant in Rangeley, which bills itself the same way (see Chapter 4). Perry is also the address for the Pleasant Point Indian Reservation of the Passamaquoddy tribe. With lupines bright on the side of the road, we turn right here for State 190 to Eastport.

The reservation occupies both sides of the road. There's a museum, and a great gathering festival on the second weekend of August known as Passamaquoddy Indian Days. An earlier trip to Eastport coincided with this dance festival, which draws both Native Americans and nonnatives from quite a distance.

On that Sunday, eyes ignored the soaring view out to the islands of Cobscook Bay to remain riveted on the line of figures offering the Passamaquoddy welcoming dance. At the head of the snaking line were the rather portly seniors of the tribe, followed by the generations, ending with a scrawl of little girls barely able to walk a straight line. Later, a tiny child, no older than four, eagerly fluttered his wings as he danced the Eagle Dance with his father.

This festival is a revival. When Joseph A. Nicholas began it again in 1965, he had to rely on Clara Neptune Keezer, a noted basketmaker, to teach the dances that most had forgotten. Clara has a home on the southern portion of the reservation, where she sits daily, continuing an ancient process of weaving strips of white ash that have been pounded out of the trunk of white ash trees and dyed brilliant reds, yellows, blues, and greens. A modest woman, she nevertheless proudly displays awards received from the state for maintaining an essential tradition. It's an evolving tradition, too. She is most known for whimsical "fancy baskets" shaped as strawberries, blueberries, even pumpkins.

Visitors are welcome at the museum on the reservation. They are also welcome to find their way to Clara's door to see if she or her equally innovative basketmaking son, Rocky, is home.

On this afternoon, Clara has few baskets to show us—most are in stores and galleries—but we watch as her short, squat hands shave spirals of wood from a pile of splints curling out of a black plastic bag. Then she twists the splints with precise, even motions, turning these loose strips of brown ash—piles of hardwood—into baskets of lace.

Clara learned basketry by watching her grandmother at a time when baskets brought many Passamaquoddy extra money. "I'd use her trash, and I kept on doing that until I learned," says Clara. She began by selling bookmarks for dance money—two dozen bookmarks would get her up to Calais and into the dance. Now, she says, she dreams of new shapes and colors almost every night—"but I forget them by morning." She smiles, her almond-shaped eyes crinkling to almost nothing in her broad face.

Now we plunge toward Cobscook Bay, driving down the long causeway over Moose Island. Did I say I couldn't take more in? This causeway passes over an absolutely radiant vista of inlets and islands. I want to fly or canoe or sail and also to simply settle down in a hollow to quietly rest among the rich blue-green of the water, or gaze out to the islands where fir trees rise straight and tall above the rocks. Over and over, while I remain in this region, my heart is torn by the beauty of this tangle of island, rock, and water.

But Eastport calls us, so I drive straight downhill into town, not stopping until I reach the harbor. I park the car on the docks, and Daniel and I go exploring. It is low tide and the pilings tower above us, perhaps twenty feet high. Within the sheltered pier are trawlers, with nets for shrimp and possibly herring. There's a father fishing with his little girl, and a young boy, around ten, who is fishing with a girl who towers a full head over him. Pretty soon, Mike, the boy, calls us to see a catfish he has just reeled in; it looks like a miniature version of *Jurassic Park's* poison-spitting dinosaur. I don't know how, but Daniel worms the fishing rod away from Mike, who spends the next hour instructing him in the techniques of fishing (mostly on how not to snag the hook on some other boat's nets in this very crowded harbor). Then he takes him on a walk to view the wonders of the tides.

If I were looking for a simpler time, I would say I have found something of it in the kindness, competence, and liberty of this boy. His life seems to be the stuff of boyhood dreams—days of exploration on the docks, evenings in the local pool hall, which is where we next run into him and his companion. We see them yet again the next morning, the girl purchasing a new hook for Mike's fishing rod.

I spirit Daniel away from the docks and over to dinner at La Sardina Loca, one of the most exuberant restaurants in Maine. Strands of holiday lights hang everywhere—red-pepper lights, poinsettia lights, baby jack-o'-lantern lights, colored lights hanging from a Christmas tree that itself hangs upside down in the center of the restaurant.

"What goes up never comes down," comments the owner, Charles Maggiani, a Marine Corps retiree from San Diego, California, who attributes the decor—Saint Patrick's Day balloons knocking against Christmas trees—to his wife, Valerie.

The restaurant livens up Eastport's main street, Water Street, a mixture of local stores, renovations catering to travelers, and storefronts that are yet to be used. Across the street is Cap'n T's, a hamburger and fish place decorated in contemporary wooden elegance, with an outdoor patio overlooking the harbor. Down the road is the Waco Diner, serving big breakfasts.

Eastport is a town pulling itself up by its fishing boots. Once a thriving deepwater shipping port, later the sardine capital of the world, Eastport entered a depression when that industry bottomed out. It is now recovering through Atlantic salmon hatcheries, sea urchin diving, a fiber extrusion plant, tourist lures, and the Mearl Corporation, which uses Atlantic herring scales to make opalescence, the iridescence found in paint, nail polish, and other glittery substances. The company says it doesn't give tours, though I was told I could come and look.

The port of Eastport is also doing well. A 1990 report that the port would handle only 20,000 tons of cargo a year was proven wrong by 900 percent. It was actually handling 180,000 tons, and that was raised to 213,000 by 1992, making Eastport the third largest port in Maine, behind Portland and Searsport. Unlike Searsport, Eastport (along with Machiasport) refused a refinery because it did not want to threaten its fishing industry with oil tankers.

Eastport also has an arts center, with a theater, a wide range of classes, and a gallery for local artists. The center also periodically brings in artists from out of town. A New York dancer has been teaching here for three weeks, and it is the culminating recital that we are now going to see. The recital proves to be a mixture of themes from both lives, with an emphasis on Passamaquoddy tradition, presented by the children with delightful candor. According to Alberta Hunter, director of the arts center, the most important result of the residency has been the links forged between Eastport and the reservation, which traditionally have kept to their separate lives.

After the recital, Daniel and I find our way to the Todd House, a 1775 cape that inn owner Ruth M. McInnis restored, allowing for electric lights and plumbing but otherwise keeping the original size and shape of the rooms. I feel like a young child of the Revolution in a waist-high bed in our tiny room—made still smaller by the slope of the ceiling above us—tucked between the outer wall and an impossibly steep staircase. In the morning, hot muffins and cold cereal await us downstairs in front of a massive eighteenth-century cooking fireplace.

After a walk through downtown, we take a quick car tour of Eastport. Among some breathtaking vistas of the bay and Campobello bridge in the distance, I see a young bride going off to her wedding dressed in shiny white satin with the packing creases still evident in the cloth. A barracks museum tells the story of the occupation of Eastport by the British during the War of 1812. Previous to that time, when Jefferson ordered an embargo on all foreign shipping, Eastport's smuggling operations with nearby Canada burgeoned. For a brief moment, Eastport was the busiest port in the nation.

Leaving town, we stop at Raye's Mustard. When the flag is raised, visitors can tour the mustard factory, with its four water-powered grinding stones, kept low-tech to keep the mustard on low heat. But the flag seldom rises on weekends. Instead, Nancy Raye reinforces our desire to see the Pembroke Reversing Falls, so we head out, turning left on US 1 and left again in Pembroke.

On the Leighton Neck Road, we pass a totem-pole carver on one side, an inlet on the other, and more than a town's usual share of hip-roofed homes, those two-storied houses with roofs composed of four triangles coming together, frequently in a central chimney. Perhaps these substantial homes, standing among wind-tossed fields of fading lupine, were the result of mid-nineteenth-century prosperity, when the Pembroke Iron Company produced an uncommonly high grade of iron. We watch carefully for a handwritten sign on a dirt road that will carry us across the narrow peninsula where we will turn left. Yes, this park is for real, despite the unpromising passage. The road even returns to pavement.

Reversing Falls Park is a phenomenon of the great tidal change of Cobscook Bay. The squeeze of the tides through the narrow channel formed by Mahar Point and Falls Island causes not only rapids, as we've seen in the Blue Hill region (see Chapter 7), but great, swirling moss-green whirlpools. There are hiking trails throughout the park. As with other reversing falls, the action happens during the two hours around the change of tide.

We now retrace our path back to US 1, having first tried to go directly up the peninsula. Don't. The road narrows to two tracks through a field.

Driving south now on US 1, we pass two bicyclists across the road from us, traveling north in neon green shirts, their strokes exactly timed. A short distance behind them comes a third cyclist in a shirt of tiger stripes, feet moving to a different beat.

We take a left onto State 189 for Lubec, a sunny, cheery town with its bright white houses. There's not much left downtown after the decline of the sardine industry, although R. J. Peacock Canning Company still processes sardines here. The Old Sardine Village Museum, open seasonally, recalls the day when a bell would announce the arrival of a sardine boat, and workers would stream to the factory—an event once common all along the coast.

Should we wish to leave this town, or even the state or the country, we could cross the Roosevelt Campobello International Bridge to New Brunswick's Campobello Island, where Franklin Delano Roosevelt's childhood summer home is open to visitors.

Instead, we leave Lubec on South Lubec Road, passing Barrier Beach, an extensive tidal mudflat, famous among bird-watchers as a shorebird staging area where far-flung birds gather in late summer for the autumnal migration south. Since it's spring, we stop instead for a walk along the cliffs of Quoddy Head State Park, the most easterly point in the United States. The squat, candy-striped lighthouse is but a

The candy-striped lighthouse at West Quoddy Head

small part of the grandeur of this walk through lichen-covered forests, past gnarled ghosts of trees, and cliffs so sheer that the mind invariably dives off, taking the breath away. The rusty cliffs of Grand Manan are easily visible across the bay on a clear day.

Continuing south, we take the dirt road from West Quoddy Head to South Trescott, found by not turning left with the South Lubec Road, but staying straight ahead.

The road is graded and dirt for only about three miles through back meadows arching out to views of rock and trees and one tiny island in the bay, where one scrawny tree grows. I scare a partridge from behind a rock as I continue south at South Trescott, though the road sign says "State 191 N." I want to linger on this brilliant blue bay, especially around Bailey's Mistake and Moose Cove. Bailey may have made a mistake, or he may have simply accepted providence: a captain, he sailed his four-masted schooner with a load of lumber into the Quoddy Narrows, heading for Lubec—but he was off by six miles. When the ship ran aground, he used the lumber to build a community.

Arriving at Cutler from the east, we drive alongside public reserve land aimed at preserving this coast for the future. From this direction, there's no sign of the naval radio station towers that cast an extraterrestrial presence over town if you come in from the west. Cutler is as pretty a fishing village as I can hope to find, snug in a sheltered cove. We stop at the store for ice cream and soda and watch the storekeeper, all of fifteen years old, move about the pool table. He's gotten to be quite a good player tending this quiet store.

There are walks along the headlands on either side of the harbor, including an extensive walk reached by taking a left on the first road out of town, toward Western Head. We, however, remain on the nearby dock. Lazily, I watch the water while Daniel raises and lowers a pulley used to grab the day's catch on busier afternoons. A fisherman takes his family out, perhaps to haul food to the salmon pens. There's a great deal of kindness for children in Maine's small towns, but not much to keep the kids here when they get older.

I peek in the fish shed, brimming with salted fish, but the strong odor is too much for Daniel.

Leaving town, we now pass the towers, twenty-six of them, ranging from 800 to 980 feet tall—supposedly the tallest in the world. There is something sinister about this plain of radio towers that flash red at night. Because the towers are used to communicate with submerged U.S. submarines, Maine's rocky coast has joined the Pentagon, the White House, and the Strategic Air Command in Omaha, Nebraska, as a likely first target in the event of a nuclear war.

As I promised, we stop at the carnival of rides in Machias. Daniel rides every one twice—some still more, thanks to the carnies, who respect the iron grip Daniel has on certain steering wheels.

We leave Machias at midsummer's late dusk, arriving in Ellsworth at 10:30 P.M. I park at the Dunkin' Donuts in town to write some notes while Daniel sleeps beside me.

In the Area

Big Chicken Barn Books and Antiques, Ellsworth, 207-667-7308.

Colonel Black Mansion, Ellsworth, 207-667-8671.

Northern Temperate Wildflower Gardens, Ellsworth.

Stanwood Museum and Birdsacre Sanctuary, Ellsworth, 207-667-8460.

The Mex, Ellsworth, 207-667-4494.

Ricker House, Cherryfield, 207-546-2780.

Christmas Wreath Shop, Harrington.

Mill River Antiques and Salvage Shop, Harrington.

Harrington House, Harrington, 207-483-4044.

Worcester Wreath, Harrington, 207-483-6502.

Pleasant Bay Bed and Breakfast, Addison, 207-483-4490.

Columbia Falls Pottery, Columbia Falls, 207-483-4075.

Ruggles House, Columbia Falls, 207-483-4637 or
    207-546-7429.

Beals Island Regional Shellfish Hatchery, Jonesport.

Lobster Boat Races, July Fourth, Jonesport, 207-497-2804.

Capt. Barna Norton trips to Machias Seal Island, Jonesport,
    207-497-5933.

Dana E. Wallace Education Center, Jonesport.

Great Bar Farm Bed and Breakfast, Masons Bay Road,
    Jonesport, 207-497-2170.

Jonesport by the Sea Bed and Breakfast, Jonesport,
    207-497-2590.

Tall Barney's Restaurant, Jonesport, 207-497-2403.

Tootsie's Bed and Breakfast, Jonesport, 207-497-5414.

Blueberry Festival, third weekend in August, Machias,
    207-255-6665.

Burnham Tavern Museum, Machias, 207-255-4432.

Downeast 5 & 10, Machias, 207-255-8850.

Downriver Theater Company, summer, Machias,
    207-255-4997.

Maine Wild Blueberry Company, Machias, 207-255-8364.

Rubicon Playhouse, Machias, 207-255-8628.

University of Maine, Marin Foundation Collection and
    Performing Arts Center, Machias.

Helen's Restaurant, Machias, 207-255-8423.

Clark Perry House, Machias, 207-255-8458.

Riverside Inn and Restaurant, East Machias, 207-255-4134.

Gates House, Machiasport, 207-255-8461.

Micmac Farm restaurant and cottages, Machiasport, 207-255-3008.

Cobscook Bay State Park, Cobscook Bay, 207-726-4412.

Passamaquoddy Indian Days, second weekend in August, Pleasant Point Indian Reservation, 207-853-2551.

Waponahki Museum, Pleasant Point Indian Reservation, 207-853-4001.

Crosby-Biffer House and Barracks Museum, Eastport, 207-853-6630.

Eastport Arts Center, Eastport, 207-853-4133.

Eastport Gallery, Eastport, 207-853-4166.

Eastport Salmon Festival, first Sunday after Labor Day, Eastport, 207-853-6254 or 207-853-4644.

Fountain Books, Eastport, 207-853-4519.

Jim's Smoked Salmon, Eastport, 207-853-4831.

July 4th and Old Home Days, week-long festival, Eastport, 207-853-4664.

Mearl Corporation, Eastport, 207-853-2501.

Raye's Mustard, Eastport, 800-853-1903.

La Sardina Loca, Eastport, 207-853-2739.

Cap'n T's, Eastport, 207-853-2307.

Waco Diner, Eastport, 207-853-4046.

Todd House, Eastport, 207-853-2328.

Reversing Falls Park, Pembroke.

Yellow Birch Farm, Pembroke, 207-726-5807.

Old Sardine Village Museum, Lubec, 207-733-2822.

Quoddy Head State Park, Lubec.

Peacock House, Lubec, 207-733-2403.

Roosevelt Campobello International Park and Natural Area, Campobello Island, New Brunswick, 506-752-2922.

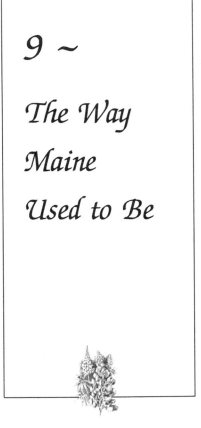

9 ~

The Way

Maine

Used to Be

Getting there: Take I-95 north to exit 54 (West Enfield). Turn east on State 6/State 155, then north on State 6.

Highlights: *Lumberman's Museum; potato farms of Aroostook County; the Franco-American heritage and churches of northern Maine; the Acadian Festival; Swedish villages and festival; Micmac Indian baskets; and a museum of vintage fashions.*

Maine presents a different face in Aroostook County. Far from the ocean, far from the crisp Yankee homes farther south, Aroostook holds vistas found nowhere else in the state. There's a vastness here that seems wild, even when tamed into acres of potatoes.

Aroostook, often known simply as the County, is Maine's northern frontier. The pioneer spirit is still fresh.

Two roads lead north and south through Aroostook: US 1 runs fairly close to the Canadian border with New Brunswick, along land cleared for potato fields; State 11 cuts through the northern forests, about thirty miles due west of US 1. Most of

Aroostook lies west of State 11, in a swath varying from fifty to seventy miles wide. This is forestland, cut by two thoroughfares only: the private roads of the logging companies and the Allagash River, a seventy-mile stretch of wilderness waterway.

I take my Aroostook journey with Daniel at the end of the potato harvest. Though it is only the first week in October, the northern trees have reached their peak. Farther south, the trees have barely begun to color.

This is also a journey to ethnic Maine, through towns where all accents are French, then to the distinctively Scandinavian villages of Swedish immigrants.

To get to the County, we take I-95, intending to go as far as exit 58 in Sherman. But I am quickly impatient with the highway and leave it about fifteen miles north of Old Town. So there's a choice here. The longer route expands our knowledge of Maine but takes us over some dirt roads.

At exit 54, West Enfield, we turn east on State 6/State 155, then north on State 6 where it joins with US 2, also known as the Trans Maine Trail. Despite an appearance of forlornness, these are important routes to and from New Brunswick and the Canadian maritimes.

Passing yards of pulpwood stacked for the International Paper mill in Lincoln, I realize we've already entered logging territory.

As in Bucksport, the mill lends an air of self-sufficient comfort to the town, which is also bolstered by seasonal visitations to the numerous wilderness lakes spreading to the Canadian border. With the promise of Halloween just a broomstick away, one house already has a display of pumpkins so large they could all be sporting blue ribbons from a county fair.

Logging trucks have the right-of-way on logging roads

The road to Lincoln leads to the spectacular Mattanaw-cook Pond, which for some reason doesn't even make it onto the AAA map I'm using as an auxiliary to DeLorme's *Maine Atlas and Gazetteer* because the miles are so stretched in Aroostook. We veer left for Main Street, passing a row of substantial buildings. A park with a playground faces the lake. For summer enjoyment, there's also a beach.

We continue up US 2 (State 6 branches to the east here), meandering along a ribbon of the Penobscot River, in this spot as gentle and narrow as a farmyard stream. We pass some large old farmhouses and a traffic caution sign with a horse and cart on it, and enter Winn, a tiny town with several false-front facades facing the street, as if Winn were a set for a western movie. Winn was the head of steamboat navigation along the Penobscot River, and so attained some importance when travel through the area was mostly by water.

We pass through Mattawamkeag, at the juncture of the Penobscot and Mattawamkeag Rivers, the site of an old Native American village. Mattawamkeag means "a river with many rocks at its mouth," referring to a white gravel bar that appears in low water. We continue north on US 2 away from both rivers. As we pass into Aroostook County, we're on a straight route where a line of roadside trees, paling to yellow, masks acres of clearcut.

Here, we watch carefully for the small town of Molunkus and the Aroostook Road, where we turn left onto an almost deserted back road leading to several sporting camps. The road briefly turns to dirt before coming to pavement again.

I first heard the name of Molunkus from Henry David Thoreau's *The Maine Woods,* written after a journey here in 1846. He discusses the clearing of the fields. Reading the passage again, I am surprised at how early potatoes came to the County:

> I think there was not more than one house on the road to Molunkus, for seven miles. At that place we got over the fence into a new field planted with potatoes, where the logs were still burning between the hills; and, pulling up the vines, found good sized potatoes, nearly

ripe, growing like weeds, and turnips mixed with them.

Before the highway, the old Aroostook Road was the traditional route to the County. With more help from Thoreau, we might be able to imagine what Maine was like when the Abenaki tribes roamed here, so revering Katahdin that they shunned the mountain's powerful heights.

The evergreen woods had a decidedly sweet and bracing fragrance; the air was a sort of diet drink, and we walked on buoyantly in Indian file, stretching our legs. Occasionally there was a small opening on the bank, made for the purpose of log rolling, where we got a sight of the river—always a rocky and rippling stream. The roar of the rapids, the note of a whistler duck on the river, of the jay and chickadee around us, and of the pigeon woodpecker in the opening, were the sounds that we heard. This was what you might call a brand-new country; the only roads were of Nature's making, and the few houses were camps.

We turn a corner, and the jagged shape of Mount Katahdin rises about twenty-five miles to the northwest. More mountains rise above the deep, wooded hills ahead. Amidst this glory of heights, we arrive in Benedicta, home of The Sanctuary: The Inn at Benedicta. This yellow Victorian structure was first owned by a rumrunner, then bought by the church. It served as a convent for more than fifty years before Jack and Sheila Hansen bought it, planning to open an inn.

The region is named for Bishop Benedict Fenwick, Bishop of Boston, who wanted to start a farming college for Irish immigrants in the early nineteenth century. Just as he began, he was given land in Worcester, Massachusetts. But the immigrants who had already begun building the college remained, including the ancestors of the Hansens.

The inn seems like an uncommonly civilized place to stay while visiting the wilder north entrance to Baxter State Park— hiking, biking, or cross-country skiing in the shadow of Katahdin.

Continuing north on the Aroostook Road, we meet up with State 11 near the Sherman exit (exit 58) of I-95 and briefly exit Aroostook County for Penobscot. Those who opted for a shorter trip via I-95 will join us here.

Sherman Station seems lonelier than the countryside, as if the life here had grown more concentrated along rural roads than in small towns—a product, probably, of the car. Soon, we're back again on the rural roads where two-story homes with large front porches imply a leisure belied by the potato harvesters. Even on the weekend, these yellow machines are toppling potatoes into bins and barns, the long chutes bright red as if from a children's book.

It's a glorious fall day, Indian summer for sure, as Daniel and I take this last, and what feels like our wildest, adventure—if only because it is the most unpopulated spot we've visited. We pass potato fields, then forest, and now a field of dandelions, still blooming as yellow as the potato-harvesting machine. Then, as we drive near Patten, the Quonset hut seems almost as prevalent as the church.

As we come into Patten, fields of forests lead to mountains to the north and west, where Mount Katahdin looms only twenty miles from us, though the road to get there is circuitous.

We turn left onto State 159 toward the north entrance of Baxter State Park, stopping after less than a mile to visit the Lumberman's Museum. It is filled with many models of logging camps and the amazing contraptions that for years enabled men and horses to extract enormous logs from the wilderness. Most interesting to me is a replica of an 1820 logging camp, a structure like a lean-to, with a bed made of straw running the length of the building under its low edge. Standing there, I can almost smell the beans, sweat, and pine pitch and hear the raucous jokes of blizzard-bound loggers within.

Winter was the logging season, because it was easier to slide—or skid—the huge logs out of the woods over snow than through summer's underbrush. Once the ice broke on the rivers, the river drives began. Stories, songs, and images of these log drives—and jams—used to be as strong a part of Maine as lobstering is now.

Maine's logging industry is still going strong, of course, but now machines clip and pluck the trees, doing the work that used to employ thousands, especially during the otherwise slow winter months. Yet even though today we will parallel Maine's most heavily logged region, we will not see many logging trucks, which tend to remain on the private web of roads, known as tote roads, inside the forest. There the logging truck—barreling down a single-lane thoroughfare at top speed—always has the right-of-way.

We return to State 11, heading north. This is hilly land, and the road rides the hills like a roller coaster. On this bright autumn day, with the hills' golden leaves radiant with sun, nothing could be prettier.

Between Hersey, population sixty-nine and falling, and Halls Corner stands an old cemetery where a body's age is given to the very last day of life. A man named Darling died in 1864 at 75 years, 3 months, and 9 days. His wife, Eunice, died in 1888, having lived 102 years, 5 months, and 9 days.

On this road, historical markers have been placed at each stop, turning the road into a guided trail. Many of the signs speak of the creation of the road, between 1826 and the 1850s, pushing into the wilderness from Molunkus to Ashland, later following the Fish River to Fort Kent.

For a time this was also known as the Fish Road, named for Ira Fish, who supervised road improvement with 150 people from July to November of 1839. The cost was estimated at $1,000 a mile.

The political cost was even greater. In 1839, when Aroostook County was formed and road construction began, these initial forays into the wilderness were considered an act of aggression by the British.

And well they might think so, for the road was built to fortify Maine in the midst of a major boundary dispute with Canada (then under British domain). The dispute threatened to erupt into yet another war with Great Britain. But the Madawaska and Aroostook Wars, now called simply the Aroostook War—or the Bloodless Aroostook War—really was bloodless, though quite angry.

The dispute was launched by vague wording concerning the northern boundary of New England as written in the Treaty of Versailles, which ended the American Revolution. The treaty spoke of a border from Grand Lake (the mouth of the Saint Croix River) across to the highlands dividing the rivers that empty into the Atlantic from those that enter into the Saint Lawrence. The British thought the highland should be Mars Hill, a prominent hill north of Houlton. The Americans favored the Saint John River, much farther north. The intervening land was important not so much for settlements, but for the forests—especially for the tall, straight white pines that were so prized as masts.

In 1832, a group of settlers from New Hampshire who weren't sure whether they were living in Canada or Maine got fed up and declared the Republic of Indian Stream.

Maine responded by putting in roads, Britain by arresting American settlers. Soon there was a war of arrests. Then a rumor came down from the wilderness that armies were marching on Maine, along with Mohawk tribesmen. In Bangor, people began preparing for war, goading President Martin Van Buren into authorizing 50,000 troops and $10 million for yet another war with Britain. Fort Knox (see Chapter 6) was commissioned to protect Bangor should the British attempt to sail up the Penobscot. In the end, the one skirmish occurred in a Houlton barroom when an American patriot toasted success to Maine, and Canadians fought him for the insult. There was also one fatality, when a soldier fired a musket to celebrate the peace, and Nathan Johnson, a farmer tending his fields, was struck by the musket ball.

We pass the turnoff for Oxbow, where the Oxbow Apple Orchards welcome visitors interested in picking bagsfull of apples. Had the British gotten their way, we would be in Canada now, but we're in Masardis, Maine, where acres of potato fields have already been plowed under. Soon we re-enter the logging world, with a large lumberyard and a railroad trailing the road. North of here, in Ashland, there's a logging museum on the Machias River, found by taking a left immediately after the bridge and traveling 200 yards. It offers free admission and features a blacksmith shop as well as logging equipment. But I find it's open in summer only. Finding my way with the DeLorme atlas, I quickly peel through the pages as we continue north on State 11. This is Maine's big-sky land.

It is also Maine's low-population land. According to the 1990 census, every town we pass in the County is losing population in relation to 1980. Many have been losing it since 1970.

Portage, population 445, at the edge of Portage Lake, is the terminus of a canoe trip down the Fish River and its associated chain of lakes. In town, we pass a large and lovely wooden Catholic church, given the courtly name Our Lady of the Lake. Beyond, the hills continue to amaze; we see stunning views of orange- and red-covered mountains, interspersed by lakes and rivers.

But soon we see more of the classic potato barn so associated with the County. These barns are buried to their crown in dirt, keeping the potatoes cool underground. Only the barn front is visible, large double doors for equipment to move through.

Above Portage Lake, I see that someone has built a geodesic dome. The height of the structure and preponderance of windows must offer astounding views of the lakes we are passing. In Winterville, the hills seem softer, the views changing now from spectacular to comforting. Again, I notice Quonset huts.

Descending into Eagle Lake feels as though we're plummeting ahead—to the 1970s. The homes—many ranches with mowed lawns—seem suburban, so the locale has none of the raw edge of adventure of the rest of State 11. This is something of a recreation community, the home of former Maine Speaker of the House and long-term representative John Martin.

When he stepped down as Speaker of the House in early 1994, he had this to say about his town: "Eagle Lake is a town of 942 people, four stores, a nursing home, a home for the mentally retarded, and a church. It is a town of one road—one road leading to the most beautiful lake in Maine."

The view skips northeast across the lake to Square and Cross Lakes.

Nearing Fort Kent (which announces itself with a large sign: "Aroostook the Crown, Fort Kent the Jewel"), the road grows populous. Fort Kent is home to a branch of the University of Maine, and a jumping-off point to the spectacularly long and lush Allagash River, a popular waterway for extended canoe trips.

Here, we leave the northern forests for Maine's French culture. The churches are mostly Catholic; though many of them are wooden, all are grand—small but immensely compelling cathedrals. There are also more newly constructed or renovated homes here than farther south in Maine, or a larger balance of new to old homes, and perhaps fewer trailers. Many of these homes have prominent facades, especially faux-stone ones. The lawn sculpture is distinctive, too, or there's more of it: crystal balls, fountains, even a bear climbing up a rather large Eiffel Tower. And in town are the four-deckers.

At Main Street, we leave State 11 for US 1, which ends—or begins—here, stretching 2,209 miles to Key West, Florida, as a Main Street sign explains.

A few years ago, C. Stewart Doty, a history professor at the University of Maine, took the challenge of comparing present-day Aroostook County with its post-Depression past in a book called *Acadian Hard Times: The Farm Security Administration in Maine's St. John Valley, 1940–1943*. The comparison reveals a lot about our impressions of history. Doty uses photographs to display the changes between the 1940s and the 1980s. Much has changed, and much has not. But much of what my late-century eyes imagine as vintage is but a bareness that was frequently not present in the 1940s.

In Fort Kent, two contrasting photos of Main Street include an imposing sign on a large, billboard-like false front. The sign announces the general store supplying, I imagine, everything from cribs to caskets. In 1942, the sign read: "Alphee J. Nadeaus Funeral Director—Furniture Hardware Sporting Goods—Monarch 100% Pure Paint." In 1989, this same false front is empty of signage, though a small sign above the awning proclaims, "Whirlpool Appliances and RCA televisions."

We head eastward toward Madawaska, passing a second sign for the start of US 1, this also heralding the Fort Kent

Blockhouse, another souvenir of the Aroostook War. The structure is of thick, hand-hewn cedar timbers, with that distinctive overhanging second story common to early garrisons.

The road across Maine's northern rim passes through a rich river valley decorated with imposing cathedrals and French names. Mountain ridges spill down to the river, which is wide, low, and slow.

A zebra-striped building south of the highway captures my attention. I drive toward it until I see it's the gaily striped exterior of a lumber mill that processes beams. Nearby, I pass a family picking cattails and milkweed pods. I imagine happy children here, playing beside this international riverbank that is nonetheless quite private. Roads don't lead to this riverbank, only paths.

We pass Frenchville, a town of cathedrals, false fronts, and giant pumpkins. Finally the twin towns of Madawaska and Edmundston (New Brunswick) come into view. With the "Welcome to Madawaska" sign sporting a French flag, I know I am in the heart of Franco-American territory.

It is twilight when we arrive in Madawaska, the Fraser paper mill glowing in the dark light. With this glow, and the echoing calls of yellow light from both sides of the river, this town of 5,000 seems like a city, and I feel a twinge of homesickness for the urban night. I also sense the adventure of the end, being here at the limit of Maine. With the huge exception of Alaska, this is the farthest north we can get in the nation. I cross the border, just for the feel of another nation, and drive slowly around the hills of Edmundston while cars honk, impatient with this slow-moving American tourist. I return to Madawaska and drive through a town lined with more four-deckers to the Gateway Motel, run by a midwestern couple interested in experiencing small-town life.

The big event in Madawaska is the Acadian Festival, which begins on June 28 and lasts for about a week, sometimes longer. But though this is a festival of Aroostook's Acadian heritage, it is not a festival of all Franco heritage—not a festival for most French speakers in Fort Kent, for instance, for the Franco-Americans of Madawaska and the Franco-Americans of Fort Kent do not necessarily share the same origins. Many of the French-Canadians now living in Fort Kent and more southern New England towns came to the United States from Quebec, lured by the mills and the loss of land at home. Many of those who live in Madawaska and farther east in Van Buren trace at least a slim ancestral line back to what is known as *Le Grand Dérangement*, one of history's many dismal expulsions, and these people, the Acadians, prefer to keep their heritage separate.

In the 1750s, the British edged out the French, and the 10,000 to 12,000 French colonists living in the maritimes were rounded up and shipped out. It was a particularly cruel expulsion, splitting families and searing memories. Most went to the French-owned colony of Louisiana—becoming ancestors of the Cajuns—but some circled back to the Northeast and settled near Fredericton, New Brunswick, in the lower Saint John River valley. Then the British got pushed out of the colonies—or found it hard to remain after the American Revolution. Loyalists fleeing the former colonies streamed into Fredericton and forced the French to leave yet again. In 1785, this group launched canoes into the Saint John River and paddled until they came to Madawaska, settling on both shores of the river valley. Longfellow's poem "Evangeline" speaks of this *dérangement*.

At the end of the Aroostook War, when the border between Canada and Maine was made permanent, those who lived north of the river became Canadians; those who lived to the south became Americans, again disrupting families who even now crisscross the boundary, even several times each day, as if Madawaska and Edmundston were twin cities, perhaps like Newcastle and Damariscotta.

Some people insist on distinguishing between Acadians and Franco-Americans. I find it simpler, and perhaps more accurate, given the extent of intermarriage, to follow Yvon A. Labbé of the University of Maine's Franco-American Center in calling all people of French background Franco-American.

The next morning, we head east, past the parking lots of Saint David Church, which are full, it being a Sunday.

Nearby, we stop at the historical society. Outside stands a chainsaw sculpture of Robert L'Acadien, carved by Albert Deveau. The woman next to him is Tante Blanche. Behind the museum on the riverbank is the modern-day shrine marking the spot of the Acadian landing in June 1785, where John Daigle erected a cross of thanks.

The day is overcast and cold, and I feel sluggish, a bit like the buried barns that have become a standard fixture on the road now, barns that themselves seem to be hunkering down for winter, up to their ears in dirt.

We continue down US 1. In Grand Isle, the Grand Isle Diner advertises rib eyes and *ployes*—the native buckwheat pancake of the region. On this trip I saw no other restaurant offering this regional treat.

The names on mailboxes and stores continue to be French—Cyr, Dufour, Gil, Daigle, Sirois—and the churches continue to rise tall and imposing on both sides of the river. Of them, the cathedral at Lille is the most spectacular, but it's under renovation when I pass. Beside us, on this gray day, the road is lit by the white trunks of birch trees and their golden fall foliage.

Before arriving in Van Buren we come to the Village Acadian, a historic village museum of small buildings. It is closed for the season, but I walk around the damp grass to look inside the homes, where I see looms and quilting frames, an old post office built on the side of someone's home, and a railroad station with a dilapidated old car. The church here is a log cabin, but the vestments are no less richly embroidered than those in a cathedral. That, more than anything, carries the pioneering feeling of the museum.

Nearby is a well offering public springwater. I speak with a woman named Lynette, who is drawing water. She tells me that there are bears in the hills above town. She had just closed down a craft store in town, thwarted both by the economy and by the new malls coming to Caribou and Presque Isle down US 1, but she is not driven off by the bears. Then she talks about her daughter, born seventeen years ago that week, a medical miracle of survival, being born at five and a half months, weighing only 1.3 pounds.

We continue into Van Buren, where I stop to look in at the Farrell-Michaud Bed and Breakfast at the north end of town. It's a charming Victorian place, white with green trim and a rooftop turret. Baskets of petunias are placed around the porch.

Van Buren's Main Street seems old-fashioned but active. This was a lumbering town as far back as 1791 when Acadian rivermen and farmers settled here. For almost two hundred years, logs were driven down the Saint John. The five small islands nearby were used as a temporary dam to regulate the water flow.

From Van Buren we leave the northern rim of Maine and the heart of Franco-American culture and head south, following US 1 along its initial journey down the nation. As we drive uphill, toward a plateau, a sign reads "Welcome to Maine." This vista of golden fields lying fallow alternating with plowed fields of harvested potatoes is so different from the rest of Maine that for a moment it seems as if the sign had been misplaced in the prairies, in the 1940s.

Rather than sticking to US 1 straight to Caribou, we take the slow, ethnic route, turning right onto the East Madawaska Road, about thirteen miles after Van Buren, just after the Little Madawaska River. We are headed to New Sweden.

This small Scandinavian section between US 1 and State 161 is yet another Maine. The homes seem more modern, surprisingly reminiscent of the "Swedish modern" style of the 1960s. The barn roofs are built with more angles, inevitably separate from the houses, and often unpainted. The churches are no longer elaborate Roman Catholic cathedrals but Lutheran austerities. Villages are built around a center common, with farmland radiating from it. The names, too, are different, Johnson and Johansen taking over from Cyr and Daigle. Even the economy seems different, with apple orchards supplementing potatoes.

At State 161 we take a left. As we drive down this road, I look to my right for the Timmerhuset, a large, deep-brown log cabin, the only pioneer cabin of the Swedish immigrants remaining in Aroostook County. At the sign for New Sweden, we turn left on Station Road. As we near the village, three children wander by, one on a bike, one with a stick, all out for an adventure. Behind them, in the distance, the farmers are working—large, forest-green conveyor belts pouring potatoes into bright-red trucks.

The settlement was the idea of William Widgery Thomas Jr., who served as consul general to Sweden under Abraham Lincoln. He persuaded the legislature to offer free farmland in Aroostook (100 acres and a log cabin) to a group of Swedish immigrants, handpicked by Thomas. Others followed, so that within ten years there were more than 500 Swedes in the area, spilling out to Westmanland and Stockholm. Today's population consists largely of their descendants.

The Swedish immigrants came with the European migrations of the 1870s and 1880s and settled into two separate northern pockets of Maine. These potato fields were one pocket; the other is in Monson.

The road leads to the New Sweden common, where we get out of the car to walk around. Most public buildings are open during the summer only, but we peer around at a community center, Lutheran church, the New Sweden Historical Society Museum, a one-room schoolhouse that now holds a gift shop, and a cemetery. About a half mile down is Thomas Park, another cultural center where an organization known as the Maine Swedish Colony is restoring a historic and rare two-story log house known as the Noak/George Osterlund House, along with a blacksmith and woodworking shop.

As in Sweden, the people of New Sweden celebrate the longest day of the year with a midsummer festival, held the nearest weekend to the solstice. A maypole is erected and danced around, and garlands of wildflowers are braided. Tours of the early colony buildings are offered. Come evening, visitors can choose from a smorgasbord or a bean and meatball dinner. Another festival celebrates the arrival of the colony on July 23. The day includes a reenactment of the arrival, complete with covered wagons and native dress. The summer of 1995 will be especially important, as it is the 125th anniversary.

We follow this road to State 161 and Caribou. The towns of Caribou, Presque Isle, and Mars Hill form little islands of activity on the way down to Houlton on US 1.

A few years ago, Caribou opened a performing arts center. Using intense community help, the city decided that a much-needed high-school auditorium could be built to serve the community as a public arts center. Because there were so many hands, the city built a $2.5 million center for only $896,000.

The Nylander Museum has an exceptional natural history collection. In summer, its gardens bloom with Native American medicinal plants.

Caribou is also the home of the regional magazine *Echoes,* focused on the life and ways, historic and modern, of northern Maine.

Caribou also has Funland, where I have promised Daniel a go-cart ride. We drive through town, then three more miles down US 1 to this pocket amusement park, on the verge of being shrouded for winter. The owner greets us and takes out a go-cart, which Daniel drives until a red light motions us in. As if taking his motor vehicle exam, he obeys the instructions without any fuss. Afterward, we wander across the amusement park to play at least three rounds of miniature golf. Despite the rain dripping over us, Daniel will not quit the greens.

Another kind of amusement is offered by Goughan's Berry Farm, east on State 161 toward Fort Fairfield. We don't take advantage of this diversion, although (depending on the season) we could pick our own berries, vegetables, or pumpkins, as well as Christmas trees. Mark Goughan also has his own lumbermill, which he'll demonstrate, and an animal barn open to visitors. Like many small farmers, Goughan has found that diversification and public involvement with the lore of farming may be one way of succeeding. Goughan is certainly diversified: he'll also take visitors soaring above Aroostook in his hot-air balloon, charging by the pound.

For a more picturesque river road than US 1, I cross the Aroostook River and take State 205 south to Presque Isle. Lives cling closer to this road than they do in most of Aroostook County, where there is usually a haughty distance between house and road. Near Parkhurst, some funny Halloween figures spruce up a lawn.

State 205 merges with State 167 as we turn right into Presque Isle, a lush, green city with bike paths through a central park and a handsome branch of the University of Maine. It also has a new mall and a movie theater.

In the early 1900s, horse racing was more popular than today, and even Maine municipalities used to own horses for racing. In fact, a story goes, after one race, the champion horse was set in the seat of honor at the banquet given to honor the winners, a bucket of oats in front of him and a horseshoe wreath of roses around his neck.

Horses are still raced at the Northern Maine Fair, held here in early August.

Also in Presque Isle is the Aroostook Micmac Council Basket Bank, where traditional brown ash baskets are sold, these made with wider strips than the Passamaquoddy fancy baskets made by Clara Neptune Keezer (see Chapter 8). The strips are obtained the same way, however, by pounding on sections of logs until the annual rings of the tree separate into strips thin enough to weave. Fifty years ago, a visitor passing by the potato fields of Aroostook County would have seen the ground lined with sturdy wood-splint baskets. Bending over the baskets would be the basketmakers: Micmac men and women, pursuing this form of seasonal labor.

Only about 500 Micmacs now live in northern Maine, cycling among the labors of lumbering, hunting, potato harvesting, blueberry picking, clam digging, and basketmaking, the seasons defining Micmac rural livelihood the way the baskets' vertical strips—known as standards—set the shape and use of each piece.

Continuing on, we turn out Academy Street, through a section of substantial homes, taking State 10 south. The road moves in steps, south and east, to Easton. We are all sleepy; even the geese I pass seem too tired to honk. But according to *Maine: A Guide Downeast,* Easton was the location of an environmental border incident in 1967 over industrial pollution of the Prestile Stream. Canadians dammed the stream as part of their protest against U.S. pollution.

After the stream, I take a right on the West Ridge Road and pass an airfield of small planes, then come into a more stately side of Mars Hill than the one fronting US 1.

From here, I follow US 1 almost to Houlton. There are more bypasses, but this route takes me by Aroostook's large farmhouses, sitting like imposing women tall on the hillsides, limbs of barns, icehouses and buried potato barns curled around them. This is Maine's potato basket, with an austere beauty of its own. We sail south through small towns appearing at rhythmic intervals where most of the buildings have false fronts, squared off in blocks.

Along the way, we pass sheds with piles of potatoes, bagged or in baskets. I buy a ten-pound bag each of russets and new potatoes from an unattended stand and leave the money in the covered can. I remember my young friends from California who bought some berries with me at a stand near my home, amazed that people would leave anything on the streets without an attendant—especially cans of cash.

Littleton, just above Houlton, has a nice-looking bed and breakfast, the Candlelight Inn. About two miles below it, a left turn at Carson Road takes us on a wandering route to a covered bridge over Meduxnekeag River, almost in Canada. Stretching our legs, Daniel and I run through the wooden tunnel, scaring a host of pigeons who swarm in and out, as if trying to scare us off.

We turn south on Foxcroft Road for Houlton, arriving in town near the statue of a boy with a leaky boot. This is the children's hour. Delicious water flows through the fountain from which Daniel drinks. Beyond, the White Memorial Building at 109 Main Street houses the Chamber of Commerce and the Aroostook Historical and Art Museum. Among other exhibits, the museum has gear obtained from German spies caught near the Canadian frontier during World War II. The

Aroostook schools suspend classes while children help with the potato harvest

museum's hours are limited, but the Chamber of Commerce is worth a stop for its walking tour pamphlets and the bumper stickers for "Aroostook: The Way Maine Used to Be."

Houlton is a substantial, elegant town. Much of its downtown, known as the Market Square District, is a historical landmark, a frontier potato and lumbering town with fine brick buildings and elegant wooden homes built between 1885 and 1910. Much of the rest of the nation was sunk in a depression at the time, but as the market town, Houlton prospered.

We first came upon it several years ago, arriving in time for the potato festival, with grown men challenging each other in a raucous barrel-rolling contest. They had to roll the barrel of potatoes up a ramp, down, around an obstacle, and then back again, all the while attempting to handicap their challengers by spilling a few potatoes in their path. What with the potatoes and the laughter, they could barely move.

Three years later, I find that the bookstore has moved out of town, the natural foods store has gone, as has the imaginative toy store. A storekeeper tells me that a Wal-Mart has opened up.

But Houlton's main street still has its large game room with pool table and video games, where tattooed young men hang out with heavily made-up young women. Daniel joins them, driving a video game obstacle course and an aircraft carrier for at least half an hour, unconcerned that there is no money in the machine.

Leaving Houlton, we take US 2 west to Island Falls. We pass a cemetery, and now the mausoleum. Half buried in the ground, it looks like a potato barn. But we are leaving potato country, leaving the far horizons, for a road that meanders through small towns, past old Victorian homes and some log homes. In Smyrna Mills there's a live calf in front of a house, only I take it for a lawn ornament. Maybe I've been driving too long.

Due south of Smyrna Mills, in Oakfield, there's a small railroad museum, run by former Bangor and Aroostook Railroad workers. But we stay on US 2, paralleling the railroad tracks, passing fields of corn. The barns here are red, not attached, and topped by cupolas. The houses have tin roofs and high peaks. It has started to rain in earnest. The road rises, promising views, but all we see is rain. Soon, we are in Island Falls.

When Theodore Roosevelt was a freshman at Harvard, he was sent to Island Falls for toughening. His guide was William Wingate Sewall, who took the young man into the north woods and up Mount Katahdin. "Once," Roosevelt writes in his autobiography, "while driving in a wagon with Dave [William's son] up an exceedingly wet and rocky backwoods road, with the water pouring down the middle, I asked him how in Aroostook County they were able to tell its roads from its rivers. 'No beaver dams in the roads,' instantly responded Dave."

There's no longer confusion between road and river here. Island Falls now harbors 900 people, a large starch factory, a collection of upstanding Victorian homes, and Kathy's main street coffee shop with an array of delicious country desserts—strawberry shortcake competing with raspberry or bread pudding.

The town also has Maine's only fashion museum, the John E. and Walter D. Webb Museum of Vintage Fashion, open seasonally. Here, among hundreds of garments and thousands of accessories, is the maroon, mutton-sleeved bodice worn by Mary Alice Sherman Sewall, wife of William Wingate Sewall, when she journeyed to Washington, D.C., to attend Roosevelt's inauguration in 1905.

Frances R. Stratton is the life behind this collection. A daughter of Island Falls, she defines herself equally as a child of the Depression. The museum's Children's Room recalls her own early Christmases with a miniature tree surrounded by tiny presents, brown paper wrapping tied with cord, scarcely concealing the little used books and homemade toys. How wonderful, then, must a neighbor's black velvet dress with sequined shoulders and sash have looked to the seven-year-old Frances.

"It was like something a movie star would wear," she explains. "I think I got the seed of this [museum] then. I knew I wanted to do something with costumes." Soon, she says, she also knew she'd have to leave Island Falls. "But, I knew someday I'd be coming back. I wanted to bring something with me." For forty-four years, while working around Maine and New England, she also collected fashions. When she was ready, she opened this very personal museum where history is told by the cloth.

A photograph of Stratton's great-grandmother tells one cloth story. With an ill husband and babies to care for, she wore what was necessary for the work she had to do, donning her husband's pants to shingle roofs or trade livestock.

But one day, in the latter part of the nineteenth century, Adelaide Danboise entered Caribou to do some trading, only to be stopped by the police. For the crime of wearing pants she was levied a hefty fine.

A century later, Frances wears pants only when she has to do traditional women's work: clean the home that houses her museum.

Following signs for State 159 and I-95, we leave Island Falls, and with it Aroostook County, the way Maine used to be.

In the Area

The Sanctuary: The Inn at Benedicta, Benedicta, 207-365-4171.

Lumberman's Museum, Patten, 207-528-2650 or
207-528-2547.

Oxbow Apple Orchards, Oxbow, 207-435-6374.

Sunny Side Sheep Farm, Masardis, 207-435-2711.

Ashland Logging Museum, Ashland, 207-435-6039.

Fort Kent Blockhouse, Fort Kent, 207-834-3866.

University of Maine at Fort Kent.

Dubois Restaurant, Fort Kent, 207-834-6548.

Acadian Festival, June 28 through early July, Madawaska,
207-728-7000.

Fraser paper mill, Madawaska, 207-728-3321.

Gateway Motel, Madawaska, 207-728-3318.

Grand Isle Diner, Grand Isle.

Village Acadien, Van Buren, 207-868-2691 or 207-868-5405.

Farrell-Michaud Bed and Breakfast, Van Buren,
207-868-5209.

Midsummer Festival, midsummer eve, New Sweden,
207-896-5509.

New Sweden Historical Museum, New Sweden,
207-896-3018, 207-896-5801, or 207-896-5843.

Funland, Caribou, 207-493-3157.

Goughan's Berry Farm, Caribou, 207-498-6565.

Nylander Museum, Caribou, 207-493-4209 or 207-493-4474.

Aroostook Micmac Council Basket Bank, Presque Isle,
207-764-1972.

Northern Maine Fair, second week in August, Presque Isle,
207-764-1830 or 207-762-6731.

Al's Diner, Mars Hill, 207-429-8186.

Candlelight Inn Bed and Breakfast, Littleton, 207-532-4439.

Aroostook Historical and Art Museum, Houlton, 207-532-4216.

Maine Potato Festival, end of August, Houlton.

Temple Theater, Houlton, 207-532-3756.

Oakfield Railroad Museum, Oakfield, 207-757-8575.

Webb Museum of Vintage Fashion, Island Falls, 207-862-3797.

Kathy's Restaurant, Island Falls, 207-463-2727.

Bibliography

Beard, Frank A., and Bette A. Smith. *Maine's Historic Places: Properties on the National Register of Historic Places.* Camden, ME: Down East Books, 1982.

Bennett, Randall H. *Oxford County, Maine: A Guide to Its Historic Architecture,* Bethel, ME: Oxford County Historic Resource Survey, 1984.

Carpenter, Bill. *Rain.* Boston, MA: Northeastern University Press, 1985.

Chadbourne, Ava Harriet. *Maine Place Names and The Peopling of Its Towns: York and Oxford Counties, Cumberland and Sagadahoc Counties.* Freeport, ME: The Bond Wheelwright Company, 1957.

Dibner, Martin. *Portrait of Paris Hill,* Paris, ME: Paris Hill Press, 1990.

Dobyns, Stephen. *Velocities: New and Selected Poems.* New York, NY: Viking Penguin Books, 1994.

Doty, C. Stewart. *Acadian Hard Times:The Farm Security Administration in Maine's St. John Valley, 1940–1943.* Orono, ME: University of Maine Press, 1991.

Eckstorm, Fannie Hardy. *Indian Place Names of the Penobscot Valley and The Maine Coast.* Orono, ME: University of Maine Press, 1960 (originally printed in 1941).

Hawthorne, Nathaniel. *Passages from the American Note-Books of Nathaniel Hawthorne.* Boston, MA: Houghton Mifflin and Co., 1883.

Hill, Ruth Ann. *Maine Forever: A Guide to Nature Conservancy Preserves in Maine.* Topsham, ME: Maine Chapter, The Nature Conservancy, 2d ed., 1989.

Isaacson, Dorris A., ed. *Maine, A Guide Downeast.* Rockland, ME: Courier-Gazette, Inc., 1970.

Jones, Page Helm. *Evolution of a Valley: The Androscoggin Story.* Canaan, NH: Phoenix Publishing, 1975.

Jorgensen, Neil. *A Guide to New England's Landscape.* Barre, MA: Barre Publishers, 1971.

Lee, W. Storrs. *Maine A Literary Chronicle.* New York, NY: Funk & Wagnalls, 1968.

Lowell, Robert. *Selected Poems.* New York, NY: Farrar, Strauss and Giroux, 1976.

Ludington, Townsend. *Marsden Hartley: The Biography of an American Artist.* Boston, MA: Little Brown and Co., 1992.

MacKown, Diana. *Dawns and Dusks: Louise Nevelson,* taped conversations with Diana MacKown. New York, NY: Charles Scribner's Sons, 1976.

Maine Savings Bank Collection. *Images of Maine.* 1988 Maine Savings Bank. Catalog of Portland Museum of Art exhibit, 15 April–3 July 1988.

McBride, Bunny. *Our Lives in Our Hands: Micmac Indian Basketmakers.* Gardiner, ME: Tilbury House, Publishers, 1990.

Merrill, Daphne Winslow. *The Lakes of Maine.* Rockland, ME: Courier-Gazette, Inc., 1973.

Moore, Marjorie. *Maine Authors,* unpublished manuscript.

National Park Service, Department of the Interior. *Maine Catalog: Historic American Buildings Survey,* with an introduction by Denys Peter Myers. Augusta, ME: Maine State Museum, 1974.

Rolde, Neil. *Maine: A Narrative History.* Gardiner, ME: Harpswell Press, 1990.

Shain, Charles, and Samuella Shain, eds. *Growing Up in Maine: Recollections of Childhood from the 1780s to the 1920s.* Camden, ME: Down East Books, 1991.

Shain, Charles and Samuella Shain, eds. *The Maine Reader: The Down East Experience 1614 to the Present.* Boston, MA: Houghton Mifflin Company, 1991.

Shore Village Historical Society. *The Shore Village Story.* Rockland, ME: Courier-Gazette, Inc., 1989.

Bibliography

Taft, Hank, and Jan Taft. *A Cruising Guide to the Maine Coast.* Camden, ME: International Marine, 1991.

Thoreau, Henry David. *The Maine Woods.* Princeton, NJ: Princeton University Press, 1972.

Ulrich, Laurel Thatcher. *A Midwife's Tale: The Life of Martha Ballard, Based on Her Diary, 1785–1812.* New York, NY: Vintage Books, 1991.

Varney, George J. *A Gazetteer of the State of Maine.* Boston, MA: B. B. Russell, 1881, reprinted by Heritage Books, Inc., Bowie, MD, 1991.

Index

Index

Index

Index

Index